LENNY HENRY'S WELL-HARD PAPERBACK

Foreword by Frank Bruno

'ELLO.

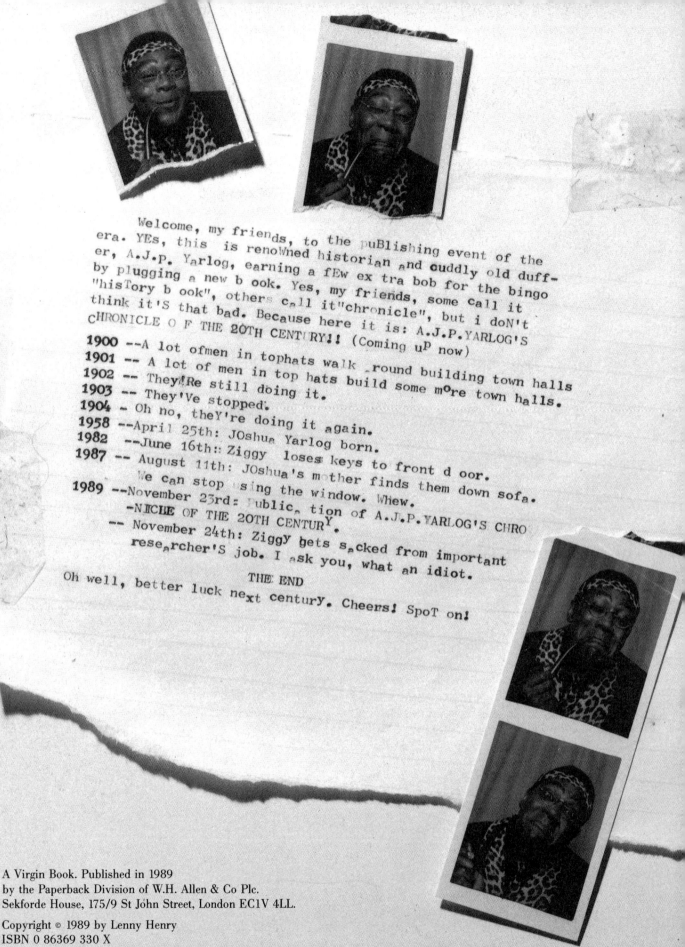

Welcome, my friends, to the puBlishing event of the
era. YEs, this is renoWned historian and cuddly old duff-
er, A.J.P. Yarlog, earning a fEw ex tra bob for the bingo
by plugging a new b ook. Yes, my friends, some call it
"hisTory b ook", others call it"chronicle", but i doN't
think it'S that bad. Because here it is: A.J.P.YARLOG'S
CHRONICLE O F THE 20TH CENTURY!! (Coming uP now)

1900 --A lot ofmen in tophats walk _round building town halls

1901 -- A lot of men in top hats build some m°re town halls.

1902 -- They!Re still doing it.

1903 -- They'Ve stopped.

1904 -- Oh no, theY're doing it again.

1958 --April 25th: JOshua Yarlog born.

1982 --June 16th:: Ziggy loses keys to front d oor.

1987 -- August 11th: JOshua's mother finds them down sofa.
We can stop using the window. Whew.

1989 --November 23rd: Public. tion of A.J.P.YARLOG'S CHRO
-NICLE OF THE 20TH CENTURY.
-- November 24th: ZiggY gets sacked from important
researcher'S job. I ask you, what an idiot.

                    THE END

Oh well, better luck next century. Cheers! SpoT on!

A Virgin Book. Published in 1989
by the Paperback Division of W.H. Allen & Co Plc.
Sekforde House, 175/9 St John Street, London EC1V 4LL.

Designed by PLANET 'X'.

Printed and bound by Varnicoat Limited, Pershore, Worcs.

Typeset by Davros Graphics.

Yow!! This is it!

paaaRTy!!!

It's the Biggy!

When you've finished **THE WELL-HARD PAPERBACK** you'll never want to read another funny book again! It's pack-jammed with gags, guffaws, and total wooferoonies, **PLUS! PLUS! PLUS!** – all your fave rave characters and, as an added bonus, the **WELL-HARD NEWSDESK,** where I tell you what *I* think, and . . .

Okay, so it's a spin-off book because I'm on the telly! There's nothing wrong with that – what do you reckon the *Bible* was? The first great spin-off! God was so pleased with his week's work that he got in a whole lot of ghost-writers like Isaiah and Deuteronomy and Exodus to put together the tie-in (Genesis did the soundtrack album). Result: the Old Testament, the original *How to Be a Complete Bastard.* The readers really dug all that sex and violence, and it was the first example of what we now know as an "S & B Book" – Stoning and Begetting.

Every bestseller you can think of, the *Bible* got there first. Remember the 40 Days in the Wilderness Diet? The Lot's Wife Non-Salt Free Diet? The Adam's Rib Diet, which showed you how to lose weight and pick up women at the same time? The first great Do-it-Yourselfer was Noah who was making book-ends when the rain started, and he thought "Hey, here's an idea!" He also came up with *All Creatures Great and Small.* Even Moses did the first exercise book when he wrote "Red Sea Walks", and in his "Diary of an Egyptian Baby" he told the unforgettable story of what it was like to be homeless and adrift in the third century BC.

The Old Testament did so well that there had to be a sequel – the New Testament, or How to Be a More Forgiving Bastard. And this is where the publishers were really smart: they got four different guys in to write the same story and charged £11.95 for it instead of three quid! But still the punters couldn't get enough of it, which was tough, cos they'd already killed off the hero. So beating *Dallas* by 2,000 years they brought him back to life – and he didn't even have to take a shower! Then the publishers put the two books together and sold it as "The Complete 'Yes, God' " . . . a trick they're still pulling to this day!

So, if you're looking for raunch, plagues and a good read, the *Bible's* on the shelf over there, next to Jeffrey Archer's *Cain and Abel.* But if it's laughs you're after . . . hey, where are you going? **COME BACK!!**

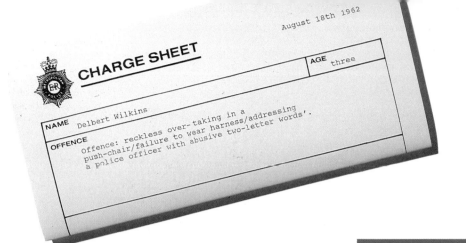

August 18th 1962

CHARGE SHEET

NAME Delbert Wilkins

AGE three

OFFENCE Offence: reckless over-taking in a
push-chair/failure to wear harness/addressing
a police officer with abusive two-letter words'.

Exhibit 1

My first arrest, guys. Busting the infant Delbert Wilkins gave them the idea for compulsory seat-belts in the 1980s. I got off with a warning, but had my cap-gun and ammo impounded. They'll probably still have them as you read this in the 22nd century! What about an amnesty?

Exhibit 2

The first known photographic record of the Brixton Posse. This was how Winston and I met. He was already inside the Photo-Me booth taking it apart to find out how it worked. I needed a quick photo for my 'Man From U.N.C.L.E.' I.D. card. *The Man From U.N.C.L.E.* was a wicked spy series in the 60s, and Ilya Kuriakin wore the coolest black turtle-neck. It's probably being shown on satellite TV to you guys now!

the Delbert
Wilkins
TIME CAPSULE

Intro

Here we present a selection of exhibits which are to be buried in a time capsule on Camberwell Green so that future generations may one day know more about the enigma of Delbert Wilkins, perhaps the most famous Brixtonian in the late 20th century. So take a last glimpse with us now at these truly memorable "Milestones on the Road to Cruciality", with the comments that the great man himself has made for posterity.

Exhibit 3

The proceeds from my first business deal – I swapped Kevin Briggs the camera from a Photo-Me booth for this single and Stevie Wonder's autograph. When I found out that Stevie had been blind from birth, I force-fed Kevin the camera. As I write this now, 25 years later, his bum still flashes four times a minute! At least you'll know where he's buried!

nice to See ya Little 'Stevie Wonder'

Exhibit 5

Delbert Wilkins introduced the concept of Flared Trousers – a bizarre fashion 'blip' of the 1970s – to the Stockwell Road Secondary Modern school uniform. Two hundred fellow pupils followed suit and every official Union Jack in South London disappeared overnight.

DIANA ROSS

Exhibit 4

My first crush – Diana Ross left The Supremes (a popular all-girl singing group) and became sexy at the same time Delbert Wilkins came 'on-stream', if you know what I mean. We were made for one another. But she went and married Berry Gordy who owned Motown Records. All *I* owned was a few Motown records. The weird thing is – the older Diana Ross gets, the sexier she looks. If she's still around now – watch out!

Exhibit 6

Winston made me this Jackson Five wig in the school biology lab. I didn't ask too many questions, but it used to move every time I passed the pet shop! The lead singer, Michael Jackson, went on to become a megastar, and is probably still alive in the 22nd century thanks to advanced refrigeration techniques.

Exhibit 10

After the Exhibit 9 fiasco, I commissioned an X-ray to look for the missing brain of 'homo Winstonis'. What they found was an Egyptian satellite dish from approximately the 4th century BC, lagged by a rolled-up copy of *Sunday Sport* (still popular, no doubt). Can you guys throw some light on it? Was Winston really a genius?

Exhibit 9

Some guys wore boxer shorts, Delbert Wilkins sported a pair of real trunks, as worn by my very good friend Muhammad Ali. How did I get them? Simple – I asked Winston to order me a box of shirts from Giorgio Armani . . . You can guess the rest. Well, maybe you can't – Muhammad Ali was a boxer, right; Armani a famous designer, and Winston – well take a look at this . . .

Exhibit 7

We all make one mistake growing up – here are two of them. More platforms than Clapham Junction. They were meant to go with my flared trousers. I have bequeathed them to you in the future so that this vile footwear experiment may never be repeated.

Exhibit 8

My first major freebie. I bumped into this major, mystical soul band when they were levitating one night down at Gulliver's (a night-club). We were all in the bog, when I trapped my hand in the towel-roll and yelled 'Bah-Dee-Ah!' They liked it so much, the rest is history. Well to you it is . . .

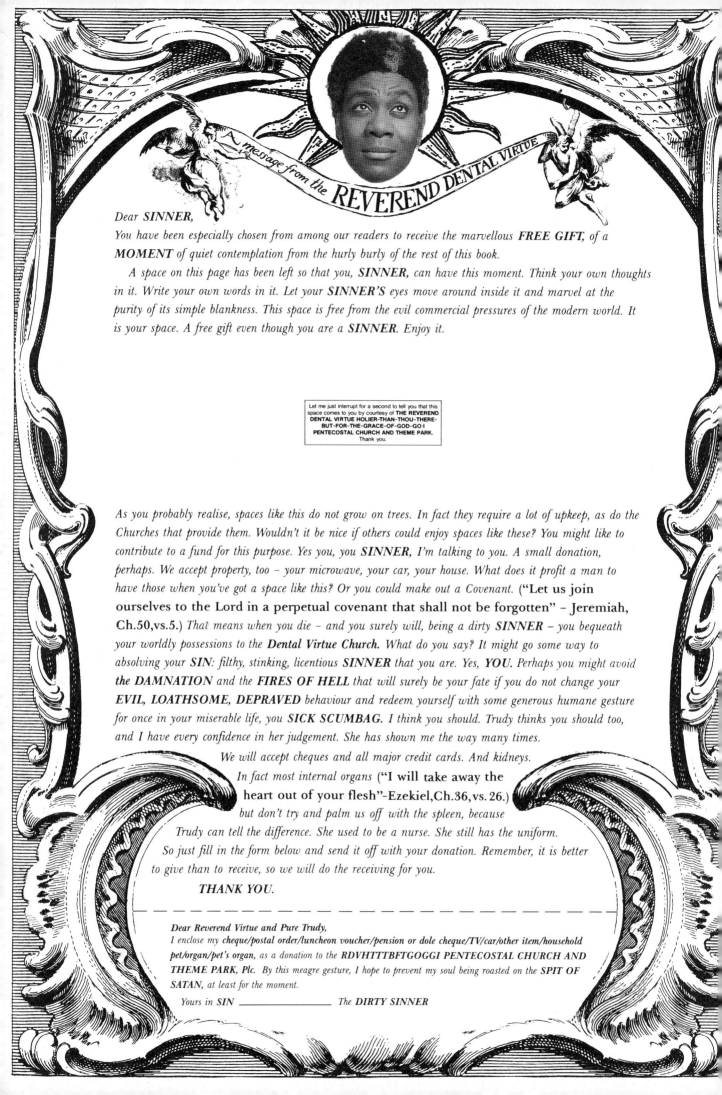

A message from the REVEREND DENTAL VIRTUE

Dear **SINNER**,

You have been especially chosen from among our readers to receive the marvellous **FREE GIFT**, of a **MOMENT** of quiet contemplation from the hurly burly of the rest of this book.

A space on this page has been left so that you, **SINNER**, can have this moment. Think your own thoughts in it. Write your own words in it. Let your **SINNER'S** eyes move around inside it and marvel at the purity of its simple blankness. This space is free from the evil commercial pressures of the modern world. It is your space. A free gift even though you are a **SINNER**. Enjoy it.

> Let me just interrupt for a second to tell you that this space comes to you by courtesy of **THE REVEREND DENTAL VIRTUE HOLIER-THAN-THOU-THERE-BUT-FOR-THE-GRACE-OF-GOD-GO-I PENTECOSTAL CHURCH AND THEME PARK.**
> Thank you.

As you probably realise, spaces like this do not grow on trees. In fact they require a lot of upkeep, as do the Churches that provide them. Wouldn't it be nice if others could enjoy spaces like these? You might like to contribute to a fund for this purpose. Yes you, you **SINNER**, I'm talking to you. A small donation, perhaps. We accept property, too – your microwave, your car, your house. What does it profit a man to have those when you've got a space like this? Or you could make out a Covenant. (**"Let us join ourselves to the Lord in a perpetual covenant that shall not be forgotten"** – Jeremiah, Ch.50,vs.5.) That means when you die – and you surely will, being a dirty **SINNER** – you bequeath your worldly possessions to the **Dental Virtue Church**. What do you say? It might go some way to absolving your **SIN**: filthy, stinking, licentious **SINNER** that you are. Yes, **YOU**. Perhaps you might avoid **the DAMNATION** and the **FIRES OF HELL** that will surely be your fate if you do not change your **EVIL, LOATHSOME, DEPRAVED** behaviour and redeem yourself with some generous humane gesture for once in your miserable life, you **SICK SCUMBAG**. I think you should. Trudy thinks you should too, and I have every confidence in her judgement. She has shown me the way many times.

We will accept cheques and all major credit cards. And kidneys.

In fact most internal organs (**"I will take away the heart out of your flesh"**-Ezekiel,Ch.36,vs. 26.)

but don't try and palm us off with the spleen, because Trudy can tell the difference. She used to be a nurse. She still has the uniform.

So just fill in the form below and send it off with your donation. Remember, it is better to give than to receive, so we will do the receiving for you.

THANK YOU.

- -

Dear Reverend Virtue and Pure Trudy,
I enclose my **cheque/postal order/luncheon voucher/pension or dole cheque/TV/car/other item/household pet/organ/pet's organ**, as a donation to the **RDVHTTTBFTGOGGI PENTECOSTAL CHURCH AND THEME PARK, Plc.** By this meagre gesture, I hope to prevent my soul being roasted on the **SPIT OF SATAN**, at least for the moment.

Yours in **SIN** _____ The **DIRTY SINNER**

BLACK ROLE-MODELS

The **WELL-HARD NEWSDESK** is pleased to bring you this Special Report on black role models in society - are there enough of them for black kids to relate to? Are they related to them already, and if so do their mothers know about this?

Why do black kids think that people like Father Christmas and God are white and look like Douglas Hurd with a beard?

In a Well-Hard Survey, six out of ten black schoolchildren thought that Douglas Hurd was God; three out of ten thought God was Captain Birdseye; and only one out of ten - a cheeky chap called Fidel Williams, aged six - correctly spotted that Father Christmas should really be black. One out of one Douglas Hurds thought Douglas Hurd was God.

Why are there no aborigines popping in for a cup of tea in Ramsey Street?

All right, maybe aborigines are frightened off by hearing Kylie and Jason sing, and maybe they're still suffering from the trauma of what Rolf Harris did to their music - but you can't call a show 'Neighbours' if it doesn't feature people who've been in the country for thousands of years before the white guys! 'White Colonialist Supremacists' would be more accurate, but it'd be tough to get into a catchy tune.

Why do no black people ever come into 'Cheers' bar?

Boston's supposed to be a cosmopolitan city but you only ever see a few black people muttering in the background of the programme. No black politician or singer or sportsman ever wanders in and says 'Hey, does this bar have a colour bar or what, man?' And 'Fetch me a drink, whitey!' or, 'Norm, my fat man, wha's happnin'?' In fact, black people usually only get non-speaking parts on both British and American TV - the five most popular are:

1. **Suspect in 'Crime-Stoppers'**

2. **Suspect in 'Miami Vice'**

3. **Pimp in 'Miami Vice'**

4. **Suspect in 'Antiques Roadshow'**

5. **Limbo dancer in commercials for low-fat spreads for anxious, white coronary cases**

How can we change all this?

By insisting on telling it like it was and is - for instance people look at this painting by William Hogarth and say 'Hey, look - a black dude in England in 1745!' They ought to know that the dude *is* William Hogarth doing a Hitchcock and appearing in his own painting!

We've got to get Florence Nightingale off the ten pound notes and install West Indian nurse Mary Seacole onto the *hundred* pound notes, cos she saved ten times as many people in The Crimean War! Flo only did a 10 to 2 shift for BUPA patients, leaving Mary to do the night-shift for the kids who couldn't pay the charge for the Light Brigade.

We've got to tell the kids how Sidney Bechet came over from America and won the First World War by getting the Germans to boogie to his clarinet playing, allowing the French and British to round them up.

And we've got to tell them about Louis Armstrong, James Baldwin, Samuel Coleridge-Taylor, Martin Luther King, C. L. R. James, Nelson Mandela, Joe Louis, Miles Davis and hundreds of others in the Well-Hard Hall of Fame!

DEAKUS' WAR DIARIES

6th March 1940

They haven't. But they still treated me with respect – when I went into the pub some of them said "You can't sit there, Squire". I tried to argue I was just the same as them, but they insisted I sat in my own special place of honour, in the corner. It was fine, as long as the darts didn't drop into my Guinness.

30th March 1940

Made friends with an English soldier called Charlie. He tried some ganja for the first time. He stayed up on the ceiling all day, then at two o'clock in the morning when the effects wore off he fell down and woke everyone up.

14th April 1940

Bayonet practice. All day running up and bayonetting a sack. I'm getting good at this. I killed 32 sacks this morning. As long as any German soldier I meet is hanging from a piece of rope by his feet, I'll be OK.

13th January 1939

Got up. Decided I wanted to see the world. Put on a clean shirt and joined the Army.

4th September 1939

The war started. I wasn't expecting that. Maybe I shouldn't have put on a clean shirt. I think the war really started yesterday, but the Gleaner didn't tell us 'till today. I hope I don't find out a day late when the war ends – somebody might get hurt by accident. Me.

4th March 1940

Arrived in England with the rest of the Jamaican Regiment. It was very cold. They put us on a train to Somerset. We lit a fire in the carriage to keep warm. The Sergeant made us put it out. It's not fair that the driver can do it and we can't.

5th March 1940

The local people keep staring at us. It's as if they've never seen a black man before.

8th August 1940

Listened to Churchill on the radio. He says never has so much been owed by so many to so few. That should teach the few a lesson. They shouldn't have lent the money in the first place.

12th August 1940

I saw the Few flying out over the Channel today. There were a lot of them. Then some German planes appeared and they all had a dogfight. I think it's called that because the planes chase each other round and try to stick their noses up the plane in front's bottom.

13th September 1940

They're still making us march around together in straight lines. I told the Sergeant Major that it wasn't a good idea and we should spread out more so we're not such an easy target for the enemy.

14th September 1940

I've been put on potato peeling duty for insolence to a senior officer. The potatoes are King Edward's. And he hasn't been king for four years, so how many am I going to have to peel of King George's?

23rd November 1940

I'm getting good at peeling. If I got close enough to a German I reckon I could peel him in 30 seconds. That's if he was wearing a jacket. A jacket-and-trousers potato takes longer.

17th April 1941

On manoeuvres today we had to find our way across country with only a compass. I got a lift with a girl on a bike. She was called Eileen. Her bike was called Raleigh. That was the man who laid down his coat over a puddle for the Queen. I laid down my coat for Eileen, but the ground was dry. She's a nice girl. Perhaps we'll go on manoeuvres together again.

23rd May 1941

Spring is definitely here, the sap is rising. Saw Eileen again today. I'm learning a lot about camouflage. How to lie under a hedge for hours motionless. Well, almost motionless.

28th August 1943

Something is definitely happening soon. We've been told not to tell anybody anything. But then they haven't told us anything. If I've tell people we haven't been told anything, is that telling them something? I'd better go and ask the commanding officer.

29th August 1943

Peeling potatoes again for wasting an officer's time. To make it interesting, I carved them into the shapes of boats and planes. Tonight we all tucked into the retreat from Dunkirk.

6th June 1944

Eileen waved me off at the dockside, crying. I told her not to worry. Three weeks late is nothing. Some of the Few fly overhead. Not quite as many as before. I'm starting to feel seasick.

7th June 1944

Now I'm homesick. I have become a Prisoner of War. After we landed at Normandy I lay under a hedge, just like on manoeuvres. When I woke up I was in a cattle truck with other soldiers who had been captured. I tried to light a fire to get warm, but the soldiers took the pieces of wood off me and hid them inside their uniforms. Perhaps they feel the cold too.

8th June 1944

They are making a glider out of the wood! An Escape Committee has been formed in our hut, and after a unanimous vote I have been given the job of decoy. While they build the glider, I dig a tunnel with my potato peeler.

30th August 1944

Everyone except me has escaped. When each soldier flew over the fence on the glider, he was replaced by a dummy, "Albert RN." Now there is just Deakus on parade, holding up ten Alberts on each arm. They are nice fellows, but quiet. The German officers don't seem to notice; the smoke from the ganja in my tunnel must be wafting up through their floorboards.

18th September 1944

I have escaped! The dummy next to me was made out of a dozen blown-up contraceptives sent to the camp in a Red Cross parcel by mistake. They must have been meant for the Americans. As I was trying to hold the dummies upright during inspection this morning, my potato peeler stuck into the side of 'Johnny' as I call him and he exploded, flying over the fence and taking me with him.

19th September 1944

Landed in Holland, near a place called Arnhem. The Germans guarding the bridge thought I was a doodlebug and ran away. I saw a lot of English soldiers attacking the next bridge down the river. I tried waving to them to tell them my bridge was unguarded but they didn't see me. Oh well.

6th May 1945

Spent most of the year looking for Eileen, but no luck. Maybe a flying Prisoner-of-War got her. I hope not. If she lived to have the baby, little Deakus would be three months old by now. Wonder if he looks like me. Wonder if he looks like some other soldier.

7th May 1945

Churchill's just come on the wireless to say the war's over. I jumped up and spilt Guinness all over the diary. Better put it away in the cupboard, before anything else happens.

The Well-Hard Literary Supplement Poet Profile

Acclaimed dub poet Benjamin Zephaniah may have been denied a professorship at Oxford University, but the mighty Fred Dread, self-proclaimed minister for the "World reggae party in a dubwise style and fashion", has been given an honorary chair in Waring & Gillows front window. Here is a soon - to- be published transcript of one of his hellfire brimstone live performances.

Spoken intro	My name is Fred Dread. The world is a dangerous place, full of lethal pollution and machines that take away your soul and run you over. I am the voice that will speak out and warn you about the dangers. Sometimes people tell me to look on the bright side. Well, I have looked on the bright side, and I have looked on the dark side, and they both look like this:

Rant

Fighting, shooting, Burning, looting, Blood and fire and death. Oh, and Corruption.

Thanks.

Fo rget THaT rubbish.
Yes,it's me, JOshua Yarlog, AFrica's preMier book wr i-
ter. You Know, I didN't ha♭e to be asked twice to contriBute to this b ook. In f‚ct, i wasN't as ked once. but
what t he hell. ♭ou deserve a good re‚d by a best-selli ng
author (i.E. me). ♭es, re‚d ers, did you know i Was on
the shortlist f or t♭e BOoKer PRize?Well, I would ha ve
been if it wasN't so D‚mned short. Some people, eh? Oh, well.
    Plus i a m so brilli‚♭t and controversIal t♭at i♭ave
had to go int♭ hiiding. (At 46a Sta♭tion Road, Willesden,
if an♭ publisher s are reading this.)
    AnYway,as a superb writer, i ha♭e decided to c♭op up
NoW‚nd then and thrill you throuG♭out the pages ♭f this
book, Because as we all know, surprise is the spice of
Variety.

JAFFA CAKES
STRING
I CAN PINEAPPLE CHUNKS
20 ROTHMAN
JAR OF SUNPAT

    Zibgy! I♭ you are going t♭ the SHoPs, BUY YOUR OWN
NOTEPAD! O♭, dear, wh‚t an idio♭, doN't you agree, readers? Neve♭ mind. Because coming up now to sa ve you time
and mo ♭ey is JOS♭UA YARLOG'S DEFIN ITIVE AN♭, YES, FAN♭
TASTI C REVIEW OF WORLD LITERATURE AND BOOKS♭ : (Coming u p
n♭♭)

    N ICHOLA NICKELBY -- Good
    BLEAK HOUSE -- B‚d
EARTHY POWERS -- Too l ong
LOLITA -- Phwoor
    MIDNIGHT'S CHILDR EN -- Good
    LORD OF THE FLIES -- Bad
HOTEL DU LAC ♭♭ H‚ven't re‚d it
UNBEARABLE LIGHTNESS OF BE ING -- H aveN' t ♭ead it
THE SATANIC VERSES -- Controvers♭l
UNDER M ILK WOOD♭ -- ♭ubbish
    PRIDE AND PREJUDICE -- Notenough rude bits
    THE OXFORD ENGLIS♭ DICTIONARY -- H‚ndy
WUTHERING HE♭GH♭S -- It h‚s ‚ stupid title
WAR AND PEACE -- t♭o long
    ANNA KARENINA -- ru bbish
OLIVIER TWIST ♭-- N♭t very g♭od
♭I, CLAUDIUS -- Rubbish
KIS♭ OF THE SPIDERWOMAN -- Eugh! Spi♭er l♭ps. Ptu♭!
    THE DOG THAT WOULDN'T DIE -- ♭ouldn'♭ put it ♭own

(I m‚de that l‚st one up. But it w‚s worth it, eh readers?) Well, that's all fro m me. Skip the next few Pages
for ‚ real tre‚t!! Cheers! T♭p readers recommend it!

A JACUZZI OF MY OWN

My jacuzzi is one of the most important rooms in my house. It comes just behind the bedroom in pecking order. Sometimes it comes before the bedroom in pecking order. Depends on who I'm pecking. In which case we might end up in the hallway. The tub is a converted Medici tomb, which my manager found in Italy. It was designed by a guy called Michael Angelo who was into sexy bathrooms three centuries before me. In fact, he probably *was* me in a former life. That's why I feel so outta myself when I lie here. It's Karma, man.

There are 24 individual nozzles to ejaculate the water. So I can share the tub with up to 23 ladies at a time. I deliberately kept it small so I could retain that special sense of intimacy. One of the gold taps is plumbed directly into the Johnson's Baby Oil plant in New Jersey, so I've got lubrication on draught. The other dispenses peach and redcurrant body-yoghurt. I smear it on my jacuzzi partners after bathing – it gives them a healthy skin and me an even healthier tongue. I think you know what I'm talking about, ladies!

bestseller. I'm talking about Joan and Jackie Collins rolled into one – whoops, there I go giving away my jacuzzi secrets . . . ! ! !

So ladies, slide on top of my nozzles and let me come into your ears with my other favourite number . . .

Big Love

Come on home with me
And drink some cold, cold wine.
Show me your loving, girl
And I'll show you mine.
We'll roll around on my pile carpet,
It's deep enough for two.
I'll mix you a cocktail, babe –
How about a slow comfortable screw.
(It's a drink, girl.)

I got a big, big love,
A mighty fine love.
It's an enormous love,
It's my big love.

You see, girl, everything is everything.
But some things aren't everything
And those things are what I call, nothing.
And I love you. I love you because you're beautiful,
And I love you because you believe all this bullshit I keep saying.

When I saw you in that singles bar,
(Yow, yow, yow)
And I put my hand on your knee,
And then you slapped my face so very hard,
I knew you were for me.

So don't play hard to get, girl,
Can't you see I'm a sex machine.
I got twin carburettors, babe,
I think you know what I mean.
So climb on board sweet thing
And hang on to your hat.
Wait a second, nothing's happening,
I think my battery's just gone flat.

I had a big, big love,
A mighty fine love.
It was gigantic love,
It was my big love.

You see girl, every night can't be the jackpot.
Sometimes you get a cherry,
Sometimes you get a lemon,
Sometimes the handle just breaks off in your hand.
Tonight was that night.
So leave me alone.
I've got to go into a small quiet room
And get a grip on myself.
I think the fellas know what I'm talking about.

(Fuller/Henry/McKenzie)

People ask me if I sing in the jacuzzi, like that other pretender to my throne, Loofah Vandross. Well, no I don't unless I sit on one of the jet-nozzles by accident. Then I sound like that squeaky clean British kid, Aled Jones. That's why the only equipment that's banned from the jacuzzi is tape machines – it would be embarrassing if the Sex God of Soul was heard sounding like some high-pitched eunuch, when everybody knows that I'm all MAN! So my jacuzzi is a private place – which is just as well, cos if it could write, it'd have an instant, sizzling

THE DELBERT WILKINS GUIDE TO
LAW AND ORDER

Five Dumb Things Winston Says to the Police When He's "Stopped and Searched"

Five Wicked Things Delbert says to the Police When He's "Stopped and Searched"

① "Sorry, Officer. I didn't see you there, standing in the middle of the road."

② "The tax disc is in the post. Probably in the same envelope as the driving licence and M.O.T. certificate".

③ "Actually, now you come to mention it, it's not my motor. It's my mates... but I don't know where he lives."

④ "Is that your five pound note on the pavement, officer?"

⑤ "I think you should know that I play golf with your Chief Constable!"

① "What are you doing, constable? Auditioning for a Pirelli commercial? Well, I hope you're insured for the damage you've done to my front bumper!"

② "I don't need road tax because this is officially registered as an aircraft. Check those tail-fins, guy!"

③ "Actually, my chauffeur handles all that paperwork business. If you insist on contacting him, he's lecturing at an Amnesty International conference on 'Police Powers vs. Individual Freedom'. Just ask for Winston!"

④ "Is that your American Express Gold Card with a blank signature strip lying on the pavement, officer?"

⑤ "I think you should know I'm a freemason, guy!"

THE BRIXTON BROTHERHOOD AND ODDGEEZERS' HANDSHAKE

❶

❷

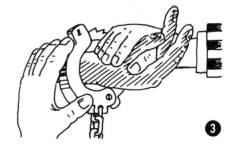

❸

IN CASE OF EMERGENCY:

Always remember that Police Officers are required to walk at four miles an hour.
So don't try to *run* away – just walk off at *five* miles an hour!

HOW TO SURVIVE POLICE CUSTODY

At some stage the Police will produce a
Photo-Fit-Up picture of a suspect who is
wanted for questioning in connection with:

**The Jack the Ripper Murders/The Great
Train Robbery/The Escape of Master-Spy
George Blake/The Accumulated Parking
Fines of the Iranian Embassy.**

It will look like this:————————▶

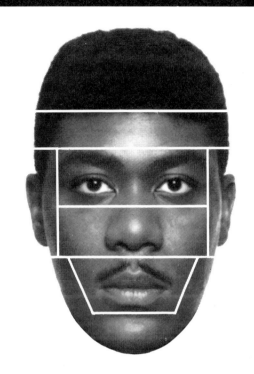

Any similarity between this and yourself is
entirely intentional. In your defence, point
out that your face doesn't actually have five
horizontal lines running across it, *and* it's
attached to a body. If this fails, insist on
your right to have new photos taken by
David Bailey or Lord Snowdon.

Confessions

At this point sample sheets
of typical confessions will be
offered to you as part of the
hospitality. Signing one of
these will, at a stroke, solve
your holiday problems for
the next five years.

Metropolitan Police plc
"Old Bill",
New Scotland Yardies,
London SW1
Tel: 999
Del: 999 extn. 1
John: 999 extn. 2

Directors: Shaw Taylor,
Nick Ross, Sue Cook,
Roger Cook,
Norris McWhirter.

To Whom It May Bleedin' Concern

I am bang to rights on this one. Stone me, I've got to put
me hands up. It's a fair cop, guv. I definitely done this
blag with _____ as my accomplice.

Signed:

X

Delbert Wilkins

Confession 1

Metropolitan Police plc
"Old Bill",
New Scotland Yardies,
London SW1
Tel: 999
Del: 999 extn. 1
John: 999 extn. 2

Directors: Shaw Taylor,
Nick Ross, Sue Cook,
Roger Cook,
Norris McWhirter.

I am deeply depressed by my committing these four hundred
and eighty six previously unsolved offences. I am about
to hang myself in this cell using a police belt which I
was able to take from the officer without him noticing. I
wish to leave all my worldly goods to the Metropolitan
Police Big Drinks Fund, as an apology for all the trouble
I have caused them.

Signed:

Delbert Wilkins
(deceased)

STATEMENTS AND THE RIGHT TO REMAIN SILENT

As you know, in order to make it easier to put words into suspects' mouths, The Law has abolished the defendant's right to remain silent. Of course, this never applied to Delbert Wilkins anyway. So do what I do – send out for a six-pack of tapes and insist on having your statement recorded, cos it may be released before you, on double album, CD and cassette.

Delbert Wilkins
Live from Brixton Nick

TITLES INCLUDE:
Don't Stand So Close to Me
Say It Loud, I'm Black and I'm Proud
Hit Me With Your Rhythm Stick
I Fought the Law
Chain Gang
When Will I See You Again?
In the Year 2525

PREPARING FOR COURT

After being charged (240 volts is about average), you will be remanded in custody in Wandsworth Prison, which the estate agents describe as "a charming condominium of compact studio flats dating back to the Napoleonic era – one or two of the original occupants are still there! Amenities include squash – inevitable with ten to a cell – and quiet walks in the quaint, walled courtyard, though climbing and outdoor pursuits are discouraged. 24-hour, on-site security. Perfect for the first-time offender!" Here, you will be visited by your "Brief", so called because he's only allowed two minutes with you. He will suggest you get involved with Legal Aid, which is a charity for keeping starving and underprivileged solicitors in work. But you can't afford this, so the only alternative is to conduct your own defence, à la Delbert Wilkins. The prison authorities will generously give you ample time – about 18 months usually – in which to prepare for your big day in court.

If you want to play for time – when they hand you the Bible and ask you to read the words on the card, hold onto the card and read the Bible out loud instead!

The Crown Court – Who Gets What

£5,000 a day
(for the Prosecuting Council)

An Overnight Stay in
the Hotel of Their Choice
(for the Jury)

£100,000 a year
(for The Judge)

Five Years
(for Delbert Wilkins, The Defendant)

Evidence: drugs, machete,
Kalashnikov rifle, etc.-
on permanent display in court

Foreman of the Jury

Other jurors to worry
about: those carrying
rolled-up copies of The
Sun, or wearing taxi-
drivers' badges, or
obvious off-duty
Babylon.

Dumb Things to Say in Court:	Wicked Things to Say in Court:
1. "Not Guilty!" **2.** "I was framed."	**1.** "I think you should know I'm really Jeffrey Archer in disguise, researching my next novel." **2.** "Didn't I meet you down The Wigmore Club one night, Your Honour?"

WELL-HARD NEWSDESK

POLLUtion

Earth's a great place to visit, but you wouldn't want to live here, would you? I mean, what would Martian invaders see as they approached this planet? Nothing, because there's so much pollution in the atmosphere they'd have to get out and give their windscreen a wipe first. But then they'd look down and see a giant black slick covering the sea round Alaska and they'd report back: "We are in the presence of a very advanced civilisation – they oil their tuna *before* they put it in the cans! Much better than our instant mashed potato."

But they're wrong. We aren't advanced. All that lead in the petrol's eating our brains away and stopping us seeing what we're doing to ourselves. We're becoming our own worst enemy – remember how we didn't let that tanker dump its nuclear waste in the North Sea? How short-sighted can you get? How else could we have neutralised all that raw sewage we keep pumping into it?

When I say "We" I mean "People". That's the word Governments use when they want to put the blame onto everybody else – "*People* have got to realise that they're destroying the ozone layer." So I stopped squirting myself with deodorant and now I've got ozone layer above my head and no friends but it doesn't make any difference – "*People* have got to do something about the food mountains." Was it me who went down to the kitchen every morning and churned 50 tons of butter? No, it was people. One day they'll narrow it down and just pick on one person – "This is the guy who's murdering

the environment." I'd vote for the captain of the Exxon-Vadez who was responsible for all those black polar bears and dead seagulls; are you surprised that birds crap on us, when we've been crapping on them all their lives?

So in the interest of science, the **WELL-HARD NEWSDESK** presents a typical 20th-century Food Chain, or "Which Came First, the Salmonella Chicken or the Botulism Egg?"

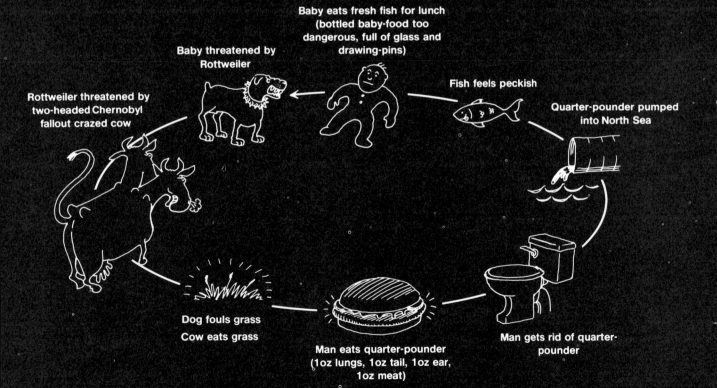

Baby eats fresh fish for lunch (bottled baby-food too dangerous, full of glass and drawing-pins)

Baby threatened by Rottweiler

Fish feels peckish

Rottweiler threatened by two-headed Chernobyl fallout crazed cow

Quarter-pounder pumped into North Sea

Dog fouls grass
Cow eats grass

Man eats quarter-pounder (1oz lungs, 1oz tail, 1oz ear, 1oz meat)

Man gets rid of quarter-pounder

IRANIAN AYATOLLAHS

Another set of guys with a serious image problem. They needed to lighten up and chill a little. It bothers me that they never seem to wear ties – too busy using them to hang people, I suppose? Joke, man, joke! So here I've given them a selection of goodies from Tie-Rack. No, it's not an instrument of torture!

SIR GEOFFREY HOWE

Now this guy needed to dress much more strategically to make an impression at Foreign Affairs Conferences. The Grey Flannel Mogadon look was just encouraging the Russians to dress the same – tit-for-really-tat. And too many arms reduction talks had left his sleeves short! The style I've given him leaves plenty of room for kneeling – essential when his Boss is about, and it says, 'Don't Worry, Be Happy!' – which is good coming from an ex–Foreign Secretary.

THE POPE

Now this guy just had to come down several notches. All that white silk and jewels were very O.T.T., Your Holiness! More gold chains than Public Enemy! Not a sound base for dissing the evils of world poverty. I accept that you look good in white, though. So I've given you a sort of laid-back, *Brideshead* style, cos it sort of goes with your pre-war views on contraception an' such. But be careful when waving from your balcony – the crowd'll think you're signalling a six from Viv Richards!

The Delbert Wilkins World Fashion Handbook   No.1

WORLD LEADERS in
Wicked Suits

Some people have Fed the World, others have Run the World, but Delbert Wilkins plans to Dress it! That's right, cos one of the greatest threats to our civilisation as we know it, is G.B.H. – Grievous Bad Haberdashery! So, here I put just some of our world figures right, thread-wise!

NEIL KINNOCK

Neil just has to get hip if he
wants to be elected. So ditch the
Marks & Sparks suits – you can
always take them back and change
them . . . like your policies, man!
I want you to get tough with the
Iron Lady and endorse the
Millinery Tendency. I've given
you leather to look mean
and a hat to cover that
ever widening gap in the centre
between Left and Right.
So take that House of Commons
mace and go on a Rap Attack!
I'll send a rhyming dictionary . . .
nation/situation/privatisation.
Dig it!

GEORGE BUSH

I had a lot of thinking to do
about George, because it's a basic
Wilkins law of fashion that you
dress to reflect your personality.
So, with Mr Bush, I thought about
a sleeping bag. Eventually I
settled on the Contra-look –
battle-dress tunic and trousers
with lots of pockets for all that
CIA money.

IKHAIL GORBACHEV

All right, Gorby, forget
perestroika, I know what you
really want is a pairoflevis! The
Glasnost Look features an
American Air Force bomber jacket
– these are now in steady supply
thanks to your peace efforts,
comrade. The Chinos allow you to
hang loose personally as well as
politically. Coming up next –
Delbert Wilkins dresses Raisa
as Cher. Wicked!

PRINCE CHARLES

Now dig this, Chas – you've got
one of the hippest ladies in the
world, even if she does like Duran
Duran. You can't step out with
her when you're looking like a
Victorian armchair. So from one
Prince to another, I've given you a
touch of the Tiny Purple One. I'll
let you keep the salmon-fishing
waders, though, guy – they're
sponditious!

MINUTES OF THE FIRST COSBY SHOW SCRIPT MEETING

PRESENT: Mr Bill Cosby Esq; financial, legal, sociological and psychological advisors to Mr Cosby; and Mary Lou Medici, the stenographer, that's me. I'm only a stenographer part time, really I want to be an actress ... Where was I? Oh yes, and also present two scriptwriters – Ed and Jack Something-or-other-who-cares-they're-fired-anyway.

COSBY: It seems to me that before we start we have a serious problem here.

ED: Problem? I can assure you Mr Cosby we've worked very hard ...

COSBY: The stenographer keeps grinning at me.

JACK: Stop doing that, we're trying to do a script presentation here. Right Mr Cosby sir, let me give you a brief description of the setting. A black family living on a run-down housing project – you know, concrete and broken windows, rats, cockroaches, rabid dogs, garbage on all the landings, graffiti, hyenas, winos falling off balconies – or were they pushed? Screams in the night, slime coming down the walls, fungus coming up through the floors, prostitutes, knife-fights, stairs knee deep in syringes, five year olds with bullet wounds – you know, typical black neighborhood.

COSBY: I beg your pardon?

JACK: Of course there'd be a few white people too, just to show that we're not ...

ED: So, Mr Cosby, there's this black family living in an average sort of neighborhood and every week they have to ...

COSBY: They've got a nice house?

ED: Sure, well, it's nice enough.

COSBY: Big rooms with lots of brass door handles and polished furniture?

ED: Well, we can always add in the polish Mr Cosby. A little rub here, little rub there ...

COSBY: OK, I want a real deep shine on that furniture.

ED: You've got it. So, anyway there's a teenage son who's always up to mischief, you know ...

COSBY: A real little imp, great. But yet he always remembers to floss his teeth. This is getting exciting, carry on.

JACK: So the son's always crack-dealing and pimping, and there's a beautiful daughter who's going out with a Mafia hit man, a couple of younger daughters but one runs away and gets into child porno videos, and the very young daughter gets regularly beaten up by the mother who drinks but you can't blame her for drinking because her husband's unemployed. He's not actually her husband – they're just shacked up together – but anyway this guy is constantly depressed, suicidal really and all this doesn't help his impotence none.

COSBY: Is he funny?

JACK:	Funny? Er, yeah sure he's funny, he can be funny but life conspires against his natural levity, like in Episode Three when he staggers around the housing project - er, the nice house - weeping and crying out against his fate because he found his wife in bed with a bottle of gin and the rent man.
COSBY:	That's not funny.
JACK:	No, that episode isn't very funny but there is a joke in Episode Four.
COSBY:	Just the one?
JACK:	Well, yes, just the one, at the moment, Bill, at the moment. But we're completely open to suggestions for a second joke.
ED:	Of course, we can always think up the second joke ourselves, we know how busy you are.
COSBY:	It's not that; you see, I kinda thought this guy would have a job, like be a doctor or something.
ED:	A doctor, sure, why not? Great idea, isn't it Jack? Every day he's dealing with a 24-hour fight against death and decay, saving the poor and wretched. And one episode we could have his daughter brought in with a needle in her arm. He sees her on the slab . . .
COSBY:	I was thinking more of a private doctor; just a few kids with sprained ankles from basketball. Remember, this guy's got to have plenty of time to have barbeques and sit around in his kitchen doing visual gags with the salad servers. And I think this wife character should just adore him and always look gorgeous.
JACK:	Well naturally, we thought she'd be very sexy looking, that's how come she can always pay off the rent man in kind.
COSBY:	Listen, idiot, they own the house. And they have polished furniture.
JACK:	But, Mr Cosby, how are the kids going to be delinquent coming from a house with polished furniture. Of course, what does the furniture really matter if the mother drinks but . . .
COSBY:	She doesn't drink, she's a lawyer.
JACK:	Always defending poor people?
COSBY:	No, no damn poor people. I want her dealing with real dramatic moral issues like talking calmly to the kids about why they should do their homework.
ED:	Er, do you think that's quite enough drama Mr Cosby?
COSBY:	Yeah, that's what I want, lots of drama but also niceness.
ED:	Niceness?
COSBY:	Niceness and cuteness and salad servers and me in a new cardigan kinda thing every scene. And maybe the sun should always shine. Go out there and write me a real meaty script like that. And guys? Try and wear some decent knitwear to the next script-meeting will you.

Guys! You too could make love like a Wildebeeste!

If you had Theophilus P. Wildebeeste's **MAGNUM OPUS.**
But you haven't. Instead – get a copy of

The Joy of Theo
Teach Yourself Sex
A HANDBOOK

At last Philadelphia's Own Steam Engine of Soul reveals why he's at the top of the Sex Charts and how he stays at it.

Between these sheets you will find out:

What to do before SEX
What to do during SEX
What to do after SEX

Answer: HAVE SEX

You will discover ★How long to make love (under 3 inches – forget it) ★ How to increase your staying power (Don't go home) ★Where to buy a whole new set of clothes in a convent school at 3 am on a Sunday morning ★How to prepare two Martini Cocktails without using your fingers.

Also included:

THEO'S SAFE SEX TIPS

1. Before you begin always make sure you know where the exits are.

2. Never make love in the path of an oncoming train.

3. Never make love in the same room as a leopard. (I always have trouble with that one.)

4. If you have to make love in her parents' bedroom, blindfold her parents.

5. If you need to make love in a field of stinging nettles, use the missionary position. If that missionary is Billy Graham, give up NOW!

"A tender and sensitively-handled insight into love-making"
– *Industrial Machinery Review*

"Phwooor!" – *Michael Ignatieff*

"Take me now" – *Bernard Levin*

The Joy of Theo

Only £10.95

PLUS! FREE EROGENOUS ZONE WALLCHART

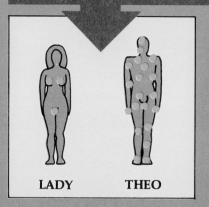

LADY   THEO

Other Erogenous Zones to Explore and Enjoy:
★ *The Stairs*
★ *The Lift*
★ *The Ironing Board*
★ *On the Photocopier (for mementos of that special time together)*
★ *President Bush's Desk*

But, ladies, don't forget the one sure way of improving your sex life – have it with me.

FOR DELBERT WILKINS, CITIZEN OF BRIXTON, IT WAS A DAY LIKE ANY OTHER...

WINSTON, OLD CHUM-WHERE ARE YOU?

I'M TWO FROM THE FRONT, DELBERT.

UH-HUH... THEN I'M COMING IN!

THE DEPENDANT
NEW RECORD FALL IN JOBLESS! HONEST!

RIGHT, GO AND CLEAN THE CAR WHILE I COLLECT YOUR SALARY-

OKAY, DELBERT-BUT I STILL DON'T UNDERSTAND---

WINSTON! I DON'T NEED THE GOVERNMENT'S MONEY! I'M ONLY SIGNING ON SO THAT YOU CAN HAVE SOME. YOU CAN'T SIGN ON BECAUSE YOU'RE EMPLOYED BY ME! UNDERSTAND?

YEAH, BUT...

WINSTON, YOU HAVE THE IQ OF A SMALL, FAR EASTERN VEGETABLE - A KUMQUAT PROBABLY!

THAT'S A FRUIT ISN'T IT?

BLURRR!

NEXT!

OI, TROUSERS, YOUR TURN!

STATE NAME!

WHO ARE YOU, GUY, A REJECT DUMMY FROM A VOLVO COMMERCIAL? HEH, HEH, HEH!

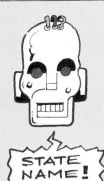

STATE NAME!

BUT DELBERT HAD LOST TOUCH WITH THE LATEST GOVERNMENT INITIATIVE TO 'PRIORITISE' CLAIMANTS...

DELBERT WILKINS... 29 AND 3/4...

WHIIR!

YOU DO NOT EXIST!

UH?

NOT EVEN AS A BLIP! NEXT!

I WOULDN'T BE SEEN DEAD IN 'NEXT,' GUY!

I THINK I GET YOUR 'LET'S MAKE CLAIMING BENEFIT SO INTIMIDATING THAT THEY DON'T, THEN WE CAN TAKE THEIR NAMES OFF THE JOBLESS REGISTER' DRIFT!

DANGEROUS DISSIDENT

DON'T YOU SEE HOW YOU CAN HELP TO MAKE OUR WORLD A MORE SPONDITIOUS PLACE?

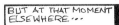

BUT AT THAT MOMENT ELSEWHERE...

TWO MILLION PEOPLE WENT BACK TO WORK TODAY, ON PROPER WAGES, DOING JOBS THAT THE NATION'S BEEN CRYING OUT FOR OVER THE LAST TEN DARK YEARS.

WE MUST PUT A STOP TO THIS...

AGREED...

I THOUGHT WE OWNED THIS TELEVISION STATION?

HE'S SO WICKED.

BUT SO GOOD!

I'VE NEVER SEEN ANYBODY VOGUE SO WELL!

HNNN! IT'S WINSTON! HE'S IN TROUBLE.

SORRY LADIES- JUST A COUPLE MORE DANCES, THEN I MUST GO!

WARLORD YOUNG WANTS THIS HOLE FILLING BEFORE WE RE-OPEN THE 'M25. THEN IT'S BACK ON THE DOLE, YOU POOR, MISGUIDED FOOLS'!

HA HA HA

I RECOGNISE THIS -'SPARTACUS'! I SAW THE VIDEO!

EMERGENCY CODE 1992! 1992!

STOP! BUILDING A MONUMENT TO CECIL PARKINSON IS NOT FIT WORK FOR HEROES! LET MY PEOPLE GO!

WELL-HARD NEWSDESK

RELATIONSHIPS

The **WELL-HARD NEWSDESK** have been out disguised as Esther Rantzen and Desmond Wilcox, to try and find out more about the state of modern relationships. Des and Esther are getting on fine apparently. But we have more **WELL-HARD NEWS.**

We keep getting told by experts on TV that relationships are becoming much harder to sustain. But these experts never come on TV with their partners, who are probably at home feeling extremely pissed off that their partner has gone and appeared on TV again when he or she should be at home defrosting the dinner. So if they stayed at home and got on with things, relationships might be that bit easier. In general though we live in an age of relationships of convenience – busy young men and women no longer get together because they like each other, but because their sexual cycles have been matched up by a computer and their Filofaxes have been interfaced to find a window when they get their cycles together. And if you've ever tried getting a bike in through a window, you'll know how hard that is. So all over town, you can hear the sound of Casio watches and Psion Organisers bleeping away, telling their owners they've got to make space for a short relationship that night. Sometimes the humans don't make it because they're delayed at a meeting, so the watch and the computer just have a quiet, Italian dinner on their own – nine months later there's a little by-product and Amstrad announce another scientific breakthrough . . . the Casio Nagging Little Bastard Psion On The Dotted Line III. The results of a **WELL-HARD/LEGGUP** Poll found that of a sample 200 adults interviewed:

124 said they felt in need of a new relationship
Of these, **35** asked our interviewer for a 'window'
Of the **76** people who said they didn't need a new relationship:
30 were lying through their teeth
26 were putting a brave face on it and were resigned to sticking with the partner they'd been lumbered with
12 were having steady relationships with household pets
And **8** were out shopping with their mothers

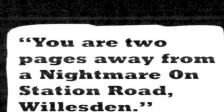

"**You are two pages away from a Nightmare On Station Road, Willesden.**"

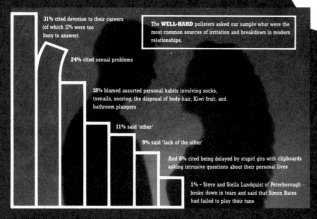

31% cited devotion to their careers (of which 17% were too busy to answer)

The **WELL-HARD** pollsters asked our sample what were the most common sources of irritation and breakdown in modern relationships.

24% cited sexual problems

18% blamed assorted personal habits involving socks, toenails, snoring, the disposal of body-hair, Kiwi fruit, and bathroom plungers

11% said 'other'

9% said 'lack of the other'

And **6%** cited being delayed by stupid gits with clipboards asking intrusive questions about their personal lives

1% - Steve and Stella Lundquist of Peterborough - broke down in tears and said that Simon Bates had failed to play their tune

So there you have it - conclusive proof that 'Relationships' in Britain are in Big Trouble. In fact, in almost as much trouble as Opinion Polls which are running out of things to ask People!

aaaRRRG!!
It's Her

LET ME TELL YOU ABOUT THE STAND-UP COMEDIAN'S WORST NIGHTMARE.

It's midnight. You're in a club. You're ready to go on. There's a drunken audience out there slow-handclapping . . . what they're waiting for is RAUNCHINESS! And you're going to give it to 'em! You stroll out onto the stage, ready to trash them with KILLER GAGS and then, suddenly, you see her. Oh no! YOUR MUM'S IN THE AUDIENCE! There she is, sitting at the back, with her hat on and half a shandy in front of her! What do you do? Two minutes of knock-knock jokes and off before she could spot I wasn't wearing a vest, that's what I did! It's just the same for the other guys: Eddie Murphy did a 30-second set followed by a collection for the Terrence Higgins trust. Richard Pryor went into a routine about how he set fire to himself drinking too much Ribena. Billy Connolly did a song about a sporran. And if it's like that for comedians – what's it like for everybody else? What do their mothers say to them?

"Michael! How many times do I have to tell you? If *that* part of you is itchy go scratch it in the bathroom. Now go and put that other glove on before you catch your death!"

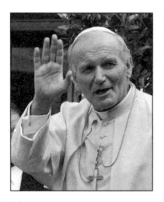

"I'll Antichrist you if you don't stop showing off and get down from that podium. There'll be the Holy Mother of a row when your father gets home!"

"If I catch you hitting people like that again, you'll feel the back of my hand. Then you'll know what hitting means. Now say sorry to Frank and let him hit you back."

"If you don't cut those nails you'll do yourself a mischief. Now wipe that pizza off your face and try on this new zip-up cardigan I've knitted for you."

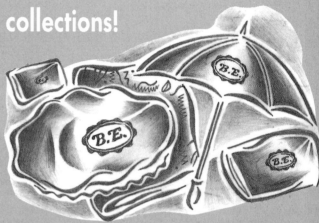

Delbert Wilkins

GUIDES to CRUCIALITY

Being a responsible father now, I make a special effort to be in by eight o'clock at night at least once a month, to put my baby son Cruciality to bed and tell him a story. Only with him being so advanced he doesn't want to hear all that Beatrix Potter Badgers-and-Bunnies-Business – he wants to hear the inside dope on the way the world really hangs! So here's an example of one of my *Guides to Cruciality*.

Yo, Cruciality – listen up! Let me tell you about the night you were born, guy. Now when I was your age there used to be this thing called the National Health Service, right, where you could get free treatment if you'd hurt yourself by accidentally swallowing a police riot shield. It was sort of like *Thunderbirds* and *International Rescue*, only with doctors not wooden puppets . . . well except for the Australians!

But then when I took your mum, Claudette, to the hospital to have you, it had all been pri-vat-ised, know what I mean? What do you mean, "No"? Everything had to be paid for, right? We had to buy a stretcher from an ambulance outside that was having a car-boot sale! Then we couldn't get past the check-in desk till they'd seen my card – not my Donor's Card, my Diner's Club Card! There was this menu on the wall like an American deli's, right? Liver, five hundred pounds . . . kidneys, a thousand pounds . . . and anything to do with hearts cost an arm and a leg!

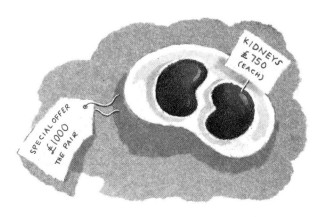

After we'd bought tickets for the operating theatre, and the Junior Doctor asleep on the table had got up so your mum could lie down, the Surgeon asked her if she wanted an anaesthetic. And when she said yes, he ushered in this dealer from the streets with a fistful of syringes, guy! But we threw him out and opted for natural childbirth, and that's how you came into the world . . . after we'd paid the ransom to get you out, of course!

So beware Cruciality – as you grow up, you're going to be hustled all the time for private health care – BUPA, which stands for Buyers of Used Parts Association, right? But remember that your taxes – if you ever pay 'em – go towards training doctors and nurses, so you have a right to free treatment, right? And all these other cowboys are worse than highwaymen – they want your money *and* your life!

Now go to sleep, man, and don't have any nightmares!

WHOOOOOOO! Yes, horror fans, enough tameness because ïi, J-oshua YArlog, Afric.'s premier knower-of-what-the-reading-public-wants, bring you the chest-bursting, bowel-churning, ~~tumble drying~~ very frightening horror of LOuisa M. ALcott's "Little Women". WHOOOO! Scary.

CHAPTER I

Playing Pilgrims

'CHRISTMAS won't be Christmas without any presents,' grumbled Jo, lying on the rug.

'It's so dreadful to be poor!' sighed Meg, looking down at her old dress.

'I don't think it's fair for some girls to have plenty of pretty things, and other girls nothing at all,' added little Amy, with an injured sniff.

'We've got father and mother and each other,' said Beth, contentedly, from her corner.

The four young faces on which the firelight shone bright-ened at the cheerful words, but darkened again as Jo said sadly:

'We haven't got father, and shall not have him for a long time.' She didn't say 'perhaps never', but each silently added it, thinking of father far away where the

Nobody spoke fo

It makes your bowels turn to water, eh readers? No, you are right, it doesN't. It is all about four spoilt br.ts grumbling about CHristmas. Which is why I will never ta-ke Ziggy'S advice again. Instead here is JOshua M. YArlog's "LIttle Women" by Stephen King (I.e. me).

CHAPTER 1
Horrible Squirming Mess

G.rrie woke with a start. he had been dreaming about some-one h.ving the top of their head sawn off with blood-spur-ting everywhere and as if that w.sn'T sc.ry enough w.it till you see what ha ppens in t'e next chapter.

CHAPTER 2
M.ggots in His Underpants

He got up and put on his underp.nts. "HMmm," he thought. "MY underp.nts feel a bit str.nge toD.y. i w.nder why." But we know why, doN't we, re.ders?

CHAPTER 3
A S.insbury's B.g FUll of Severe d Fingers

It w.s the middle of the night .nd he w.s .ll alone in the house which h.d been built on the site of . deconsec-rated cemetery by a der.nged Satanist who h.d subsequen-tly murdered his wife .nd children .nd then v.nished with-out tr.ce. A clock ticked, .n owl hooted, he opened the door to the kitchen. CREEEEEEAAAAAAAAK.

There on the table was a Sainsbury's bag.

"FUnny," he though, "i feel sure that I unpacked that
Sainsbury'S bag last night and put all the shopping in
the fridge...OH well," he continued thinking. "SInce i am
feeling hungry after that horrible dream (see CHAPTER 1),
i think I will look inside the bag and eat whatever'S in
there. Mmm, yum!"

He went over to the table and slowly, very slowly, opened the Sainsbury'S bag... It was empty.

Hah! Fooled you.

CHAPTER 4
The Fridge

"Doh," said Garrie, "I was right all along. Let'S look in
the fridGe."

He opened the door. CREEEAAAAK PING! (the fridge light
going on). AS the condensation cleared, his unbelieving
eyes saw before him, squirming, writhing, seething, slid-
ing down the celery, trampolining off the KRaft CHeese
Slices and diving into the yoghurt, score upon score of
LITTLE WOMEN!

"We are the hellsPawn of LOuisa M. Alcott," they shriek-
ed. "And we have come to SWALLOW YOUR SOUL!!!"

Eyes ablaze, crinolines akimbo, about two inches tall,
they poured out of the fridge.

"AH! AH! AH!" went Garrie.

"We'Re going to get you!" they chanted in unison, just
like in Evil Dead.

"NO! NO! NO!" went Garrie and started stamping.

SPLAT! There goes Meg. SQUISH! Goodbye, Beth. SPWIT!
Sayonara, Little Amy. Red, pulpy mush covered the lino-
leum. (You might say this is not scary, just disgusting.
Well, you are wrong.) He grabbed a handful of pint-sized
spoilt brats and forced them down t he waste disposal.
GRIND GRIND JUDDER JUDDER. As gloppy green bile bubbled
up into the sink, he made a dash for the front door.

"THe keys, the keys, oh no, oh No, fumble fumble."
"Booga booga booga," went t he horrible little girls.

PHEW! He managed to get the key in the lock. But just
as he did, readers, guess what? It was pushed back out
FROM THE OTHER SIDE!! Yes, h undreds of EVEN LITTLER
WOMEN came pouring in through the keyhole.

"WHEEEEEEE!" they squeaked in AMerican accents, and
forced their way uP his nose, into his mouth, down his
throat. Six of them had a wrestling match with the magg-
ots in his underpants. (Remember them?) They were chokin
g him, choking him, he could not scream, could not breathe,
could not...

And then Garrie woke up.

"Phew, it was only a dream," he said. "Ha ha ha."

Just then a man burst in and sawed the top of his head
off.

THE END... OR IS IT?

Yes, it is. Cheers.

THE WEDDING OF THE MONTH

It was certainly a jolly occasion when Mr. Nathan D. Campbell married Miss Marcia Jane Leigh at the Pentecostal Baptism of the Infant Jesus Holy Tongues of Fire Church Hall this Saturday morning. The reception began smoothly at twelve noon and finished . . . well it's still going on actually.

Mr Leigh welcomes his son-in-law to the family.

Messrs Lloyd and Ranking Blood provided discreet background music throughout the occasion.

After conducting the service the Reverend Vincent Almanac also kindly presided at the reception as master of ceremonies.

The tasty wedding cake was made by the bride's mother from an old family recipe.

The cheery groom thanks the shy bridesmaid.

The blushing bride asks her bridesmaid for last-minute honeymoon advice.

Greetings arrive from local well-wishers. "Hello, hello, hello" they all seemed to be saying – what a thoughtful gesture to end a happy occasion.

THE ULTIMATE TRAINING SHOE –
THE CRUCIAL CRAMCOE

Unique **CRAMCOE** design flashes in magenta suede strips give your shoe the hall-mark of exclusivity! Each strip is hand-sculpted to fit your individual hi-arch profile by third-world boy workers earning a hundredth of the price of this shoe per year!

Inner impact absorption sole, constructed of ozone-friendly recycled tabloid newsprint, extensively tested for shocks and ability to absorb unpleasant smells.

Silk and nylon compound laces in pastel colour of your choice, matched to outside sole waffle and stabilising rim. Silicon chip "Moron" voice processor in toe-flap protector gives precise instructions on tying.

Strontium-90 core for fission-powered lift and suspension. Perspex panel allows check on radiation levels and incorporated coolant-system. When panel turns green and glows, run like *stink!*

The remaining 65% energy emits laser light through twin toe over-supinators – ideal for night work-out! In-built copper-cell alarm system emits advanced warning of dog turds.

The ultra-hard, ultra-lite Zircon and Cadmium compound sole, fitted with Aluminium torsion bar, giving maximum torque and anti-pronation credentials. Unique absorbency sole returns 35% of energy expended!

THE CRUCIAL CRAMCOE –
THE CROSS-TRAINING SUPERSHOE FOR THE
GULLIBLE NARCISSIST OF TODAY !

ONLY £199.95
– OR £300 PER PAIR ! ! !

$2.50

weLL#def

Sex-clusive:

Wildebeeste Talks! (and moans and purrs)

Muslim Mania:

Abdullah X

How Low Can You Go? Finger Lickin' Hound-Dog Tells Ya!

Wacko Jacko's Style Secrets!

Ike Turner
on Tina'n'Stuff!

Plus Plus Plus! ★ The Latest Hip-Hop

Chart! ★ Delbert Wilkins All-Time Dee-Jay Hall of Fame! ★ ★ Grand Slammin' Comp-O-Tition! ★

IF YOU AIN'T WELL DEF, YOU AIN'T HEARIN' NUTHIN'!

The **LOWDOWN** on **LOWDOWN**

My name is Lowdown, Finger-lickin Dirty Hound Dog Smith. I'm a blues singer. I've been singing the blues for fifty years. And that's a mighty long time. Especially if you wanna go to the toilet. I come from the deep South. It's a dangerous place. I remember doing a gig for 500 Klu Klux Klansmen. It's hard playing the guitar when you're nailed to a cross. Couldn't get that F chord for nuthin.

Once a guy came up to me and said: "What is the blues?" So I nailed his nuts to a tree. I said: "Multiply that pain by a lifetime and you nearly got the blues." That was the last time a cop asked me a stupid question.

I spent a lot of time in solitary confinement; that was fine except I was on my own all the time. The only other company I had was cockroaches. I got on real well with them roaches; I learnt to speak roach – it's a bit like French only they don't have so many words for cheese. Roaches are more reliable than people; you know where you are with a roach. You give a roach a dead mouse, you got a friend for life – you can't say that for people. I used to train them to go out and get me a newspaper. They'd rip it up into little bits, carry it under the door, and I'd put it back together again. It took me three years to reassemble a copy of the *New York Times*, but it was worth it; it kept me sane.

I used to work on the railroad. The Indians called it the Iron Horse. They were confused by it. They'd get hold of a real horse, light a fire up its ass, and wonder why it didn't stay on the track. I used to watch them and think: "Now there goes a horse with the blues."

If you want to sing the blues, you got to suffer. You got to be insulted, discriminated against, beaten, kicked, starved, wrongly accused, framed, thrown in jail, kicked out of your house, abandoned by your woman for another guy, shot, whipped, stabbed, hospitalised, eaten by boll weevils, drunk, enslaved, forced to work on a chain gang, humiliated, embarrassed, transported and hung. When you've done all that, you'll be able to sing the blues. In the meantime, you can try singing along to this:

Finger lickin' Hound dog Sing-a-long Mississippi delta Bowl Weevil Freight train blues

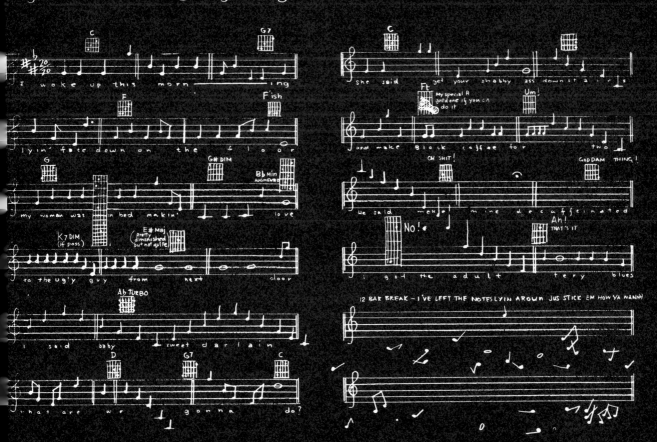

So I thought I'd go get my gun and shoot that sucker.

I went to the elevator, shot fifteen floors down.
Then I realised I didn't have no elevator
As my ass smashed into the ground.
I staggered across the street cursing my bad luck,
Bent down to pick up a rabbit's foot
Got knocked down by a truck.
Two headlamps and a radiator grill parked up my ass.
I got the intensive care blues.

They took me to court.

The judge he said: "Boy, you could do some time,
Obstructing a motor vehicle is a very serious crime."
I said: "I'll put my trust in the jury
Twelve true men and good."
Then the jury walked in: a dozen guys. White hoods.
I got the "I'm in deep shit" blues.

So they sent me to jail.

(MUSICAL BREAK)

I got twenty years for jay-walking,
Bread and water and all the jazz.
So I tunnelled out of San Quentin
But the tunnel came out in Alcatraz.
So if your woman has done you wrong
And your love has grown cold –
The moral to this story is
Just make the goddamn coffee when you're told.
And make mine with two sugars.

That's the coffee blues.

★★★★ The ★★★★
★★ Well-Def ★★

Linzi Anderson talks to Theophilus P. Wildebeeste

A chance to rub shoulders with the sexiest man alive? That's what they told me. But it wasn't his shoulders that worried me, it was that codpiece. How can any self-respecting journalist have a tête-à-tête with a guy whose codpiece is the same size as his head?

My brief was to interview Theophilus P. Wildebeeste, the soul singer who put the 'ram' into rampant, the spikey bit into stud and the speedometer into bed. Theo, millionaire and so-called sex symbol, had taken over five floors of the most expensive hotel in London – which was uncomfortable for the other guests as it only has four floors and a basement car-park. Theo's latest hit single 'Sign Your Name Across My Codpiece' was filtering across the tannoy.

I thought I'd arrived early. He was in his heart-shaped red satin bed and not dressed for callers, not dressed at all. There was some confusion about why I was there: 'I told them no more girls, I need some sleep, I draw the line at nine an hour, enough is enough, too much is enough.'

I explained who I was but Theo stayed in bed all the same. 'I'm sure you'll change your mind in a minute, honey.'

When he'd finished combing his chest hair for the photographers, Theo started to move towards me, saying, 'Hey, you're so small and cute I could wear you as a badge.'

I decided it was time to get to a safe distance and start asking questions.

INT: Listen Theo, to me you're about as sexy as damp slippers, so let's get started. Get back over there please. Now, I notice you never have female members in your band, is this deliberate?

THEO: You really want me this far away from you? OK. What are you asking me about? *Female members?* I find that question kinda confusing.

INT: I *mean* there are no women in your band.

THEO: Oh. Oh no, sweetheart, women deplete the hormone level in the band. We like to give out a very male atmosphere for our fans – put just one woman in there and the chromosomes get unbalanced, band gets too X and not enough Y.

INT: You've got to be kidding, not enough Y?

THEO: Well, I don't know, but I notice the guys start singing the backing vocals too high. I don't want that high singing, I'm not Michael Jackson.

INT: Don't you admire Michael Jackson?

THEO: Well, sure, the kid can dance but so can Roger Rabbit. No, seriously, it might look good but it's all animatronics – you watch the mixing desk and the guy with the remote control. Kid has got Made in Taiwan tattooed on his backside.

INT: Really. I suppose you'd find it hard to put down Prince so easily.

THEO: I wouldn't have picked him up in the first place. Mind you, that wouldn't be hard, he must weigh about as much as a potato chip, less probably. He must've smoked a lot as a child . . . left a bit of ash on his top lip too.

INT: But he's amazingly talented! He can sing, dance, compose, play different instruments, make movies . . .

THEO: Yeah, but when's he gonna grow some chest hair? When he can grow a chest like

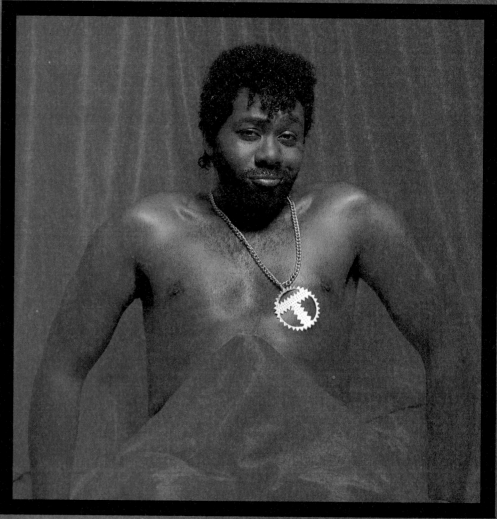

this *then* you can tell me the guy's got talent. That guy has no body hair – what's sexy about a dancing egg with arms and legs and a ponytail?

INT: He seems to be very successful without body hair.

THEO: He's just hit a lucky patch. I haven't made an album for a couple of years remember. That's how he got a chance to sneak in the back door, but he hasn't got the staying-power of a real star like me.

INT: Who else would you call a real star?

THEO: Nobody who's alive. Maybe Alexander O'Neal but he

sweats too much. The guy sweats so much on stage they can use his old suits for Third World irrigation systems.

INT: I notice you haven't mentioned any female musicians.

THEO: Who is there? Anita Baker is just Michael Macdonald in drag. I keep expecting the rest of the Doobie Brothers to walk on stage any minute and say, 'OK Mike, we're taking you home. Come quietly and, Mike, take off the dress.'

INT: I see. Look, do you think you could leave that alone?

THEO: What?

INT: My leg.

THEO: You don't want me to stroke it?

INT: No.

THEO: Well, lady, don't rub up against me then.

INT: All in all, you're pretty sexist, aren't you Theo?

THEO: Sure, I'm a male chauvinist – but at least I never have to wash-up. I'm not one of those poor skinny little guys who's got in the grip of the killer evil doom of feminists.

INT: Do you feel threatened by feminists?

THEO: Listen honey, feminists are just women who haven't met me yet. If all women

were feminists, who would bring people on stage in quiz shows? If women want to compete with men I say, fine, let's start with Sumo wrestling.

INT: You think any woman could really live up to your ridiculous standards?

THEO: The fact that I haven't met a woman yet who matched up to my idea of perfection means there's something wrong with the women I meet, not me, isn't that right? Every time I think I've met the woman of my dreams she starts wanting me to do kinky stuff. Like listen to her when she talks. And that other stuff.

INT: Other stuff? You mean equality, fidelity, honesty?

THEO: No, you know. *That* other stuff.

INT: What other stuff?

THEO: The sticky nasty bit, you know. That's not nice. I just like to roll around on the bed and moan a bit, all that other stuff's unnatural. And unhygenic. You're an educated woman, I'm sure you understand.

INT: You mean you don't actually ever do it with all your ladies?

THEO: Listen, I just have to breathe on a lady and she's satisfied. Why make a mess on the sheets?

INT: You're breathing on me now Theo.

THEO: That's right baby. How do you feel?

INT: Like my head's in an oven full of garlic bread.

THEO: That good, huh? You want me to moan a bit too? You want to get in here and roll around?

INT: How about going the whole way for once Theo?

THEO: What? Are you crazy? Hey! Where are my bodyguards, there's another of those sick perverted women in here! Get her away from me before she ruins the sheets! Help me somebody!

HAIR PROBLEMS?

LET THE SCIENTISTS AT THE 'BLACK EXECUTIVE DAMAGED HAIR CLINIC' SOLVE THEM FOR YOU!

With our vast expertise in the hair and allied grooming fields, we can advise on anything you care to throw at us!

Whatever's troubling you – premature graying, drooping curls, scalp exfoliation, thinning – the men in the white coats at BLACK EXECUTIVE are prepared to tackle it, head-on. Just send us a sample of your hair in an envelope for one of our free, no obligation, diagnostic readings. Our Head Coaches will be able to advise on your condition and suggest the BEST – the BLACK EXECUTIVE SPECIAL TEAM that will win the ball-game for you! AFRICAN 1000 for that back–to–nature blackness; FORMULA JAMES BROWN for hair that always Stands Up; MICHAEL X for eradicating white flakes.

And if we find an empty envelope on our desk, we'll know that you need the ultra-discreet services of our HAIR EXTENSION AND HAND-MADE TOUPEE DIVISION.

Put Your Head in Our Hands, and We Won't Let You Down! – that's the BLACK EXECUTIVE Promise!

MICHAEL JACKSON

THE MAKING OF A MEGASTAR

The pop music phenomenon Michael Jackson has been performing since he was a tiny kid. Who can forget that first Jackson Five hit – 'ABC', so called because that was as far as Michael had got into the alphabet. But just how did that little boy learn the tricks and traits that are so much a part of his performance as a megastar today? It's commonly assumed that the other brothers in the Jackson Five were responsible. But we have uncovered evidence in family files and cuttings to suggest otherwise. For The Jackson Five were, in fact, only an advance party – they left the "Hundred" off the group's name so as not to deter promoters.

THE JACKSON SQUEAL

We can reveal that Michael's famous high-pitched squeal came about as a result of an incident involving his youngest sister LaToya's pet hamster, Duane. The 14-year-old Michael had just found that his voice had broken, and, while stomping about the house in a deep depression, thinking his showbiz career was over, he trod on Duane. The hamster let out a high-pitched squeal – as indeed did LaToya – and Michael cried. He hated hurting animals, and he also hated losing his own choirboy voice. So he did a deal with LaToya – free cans of Coke for life – and he got Duane, who was then successfully transplanted by microsurgeons at Disneyland Hospital into Michael's larynx. Michael and Duane have been inseparable ever since, duetting on countless numbers, including 'Thriller' and 'Dirty Diana'.

THE JACKSON MOONWALK

Michael got the idea for his most dazzling dance-move from one of his older cousins, Barnaby Jackson, who had also once had a run in with Duane the hamster – he'd tripped over him in the summer of 1969 and fallen head-first into the TV set while they were showing the first moon-landing. As a result of this accident, Barnaby believed himself to be the astronaut Neil Armstrong. Several months of treatment at The Richard Nixon Center for Strange Delusions failed to cure Barnaby, and he continued to move around the family home as if weightless. The only way Michael could console him was to imitate his motions, and thus The Moonwalk was born. Barnaby is currently on a manned flight to Venus.

THE JACKSON SINGLE GLOVE

This famous gesture and fashion feature has its origins with Michael's Midwest farmer Uncle, Jesse "No-Not-*The*-Jesse" Jackson. In his teens Michael went to stay on the farm during summer holidays and used to help Uncle Jesse "No-Not-*The*-Jesse" when it came to artificially inseminating the mules. Jesse wore a pair of leather gloves for this task, but when he was unfortunately kicked into the air by a wayward animal,

one of the gloves was lost for ever. The sight of Uncle Jesse lying on the barn roof, with his one gloved fist raised in a dying salute, left a lasting impression on young Michael. Indeed his backing group now only have to shout "Mule's Ass!" across the stage for Michael's hand to shoot up into the air. Millions of fans repeat the gesture, not knowing of the distress it is causing to mules across the world.

THE JACKSON CROTCH GRAB

Analysts and psychiatrists feverishly discuss the rationale for this defensive gesture. Is he frightened of losing his manhood? Is he holding on to his money from the Coke adverts? Is it meant to help him count when he sings "ABC! It's easy as 1-2-3!"? Does it indicate a fundamental urge not to procreate and thereby retain his youthfulness? The answer is simpler, we believe – the first time he let Bubbles the chimp stay the night, Michael caught a dose of fleas. On stage next day, he had to keep scratching away and the fans went wild with what they imagined to be an enticingly sexual gesture. It has stayed in the act ever since, although the fleas themselves have since been removed and paid off with a beach house in Malibu.

DELBERT WILKINS ALL-TIME "TOP JOCK" CHARTS

AM
FM
MW

1

NAME ....DELBERT WILKINS
STATION ....CRUCIAL FM
COMMENTS ....The all-time boss. The first Emperor of funk. The long gravel drive of house. The big super-duper of sponditiousness.

6

NAME ....SIMON DEE
STATION ....RADIO LONDON
COMMENTS ....Arrived on scene driving a white E-type, left driving a London bus! Should have stuck to his real name – Henty-Dodd. Sounds like a seriously wicked dude!

2

NAME ....TONY BLACKBURN
STATION ....RADIO LONDON
COMMENTS ....Champion of Soul Music. "Arnold" the barking dog was totally wicked concept. Haircut ideal for radio.

7

NAME ....ALAN FREEMAN
STATION ....THE LIGHT PROGRAMME
COMMENTS .....Nickname, "Fluff". Why? Cos he was always at the end of a gramophone needle! Crucial way with words: "All right", "Not 'arf", "er . . ." etc.

3

NAME ....EMPEROR ROSKO
STATION ....RADIO CAROLINE
COMMENTS ......"Great Cazaboo!!" was his catchphrase – total cobs, total magic. Broadcast just as I was getting up – Saturday lunch-time! not so much an emperor, more of an archduke?

8

NAME ....JOHNNY WALKER
STATION ....RADIO CAROLINE
COMMENTS ..... Signed off every night with Percy Sledge. Got couples to park on the Essex coast and flash their headlights. Yes guys, the 60s were *that* exciting!

4

NAME ....STUART HENRY
STATION ....LUXEMBOURG
COMMENTS ....."Hello, my friends!" was his intro.

9

NAME ....ANDY PEEBLES
STATION ....PICCADILLY RADIO
COMMENTS .....Shunts his mega "Soul Train" up and down the country late at night. Despite his name, not a "Jock" Jock, and not as tall as he sounds, either!

> **This scoundrel stole it from me! He'll be hearing from my lawyers! I have spoken.**

10

NAME ....DELBERT WILKINS
STATION .... BBC WORLD SERVICE
COMMENTS ..... In with a bullet! From bad to wicked as he goes legit, and rules the airwaves turning the Ozone into the crucial zone!

DELBERT WILKINS ALL-TIME BOTTOM TEN

91
NAME ....KEITH CHEGWIN

92-100
Any other radio 1 Dee-Jays.

weLL#def.

ABDULLAH X SPEAKS

Last month L.L.Kruggerand-Chain, currently charting at 5 with 'The Poverty Scandal (Inner City Nightmare)', elected to adopt the Muslim faith and to take Abdullah X as his chosen name. Here, he tells of his reasons for the change of identity and direction.

" By dedicating myself to Allah, I feel my voice now has more relativity to the way I feel, and to the reception, persona-wise, of my image, both physical and spiritual. Those who condemned me in the past for talking tough but living rich, now stand as so many hand-servants of Satan. I now have a four-focal situation regarding my inner force – Mutha, Fatha, Brutha and now Allah. Maybe five if you count my Neighba. I can see through the darkness which, uh, you know, pervadifies through and round this whole thang called, quotes, 'The Music Bizness'. Check it out – the system only operates for, in terms of power, let me spell that for ya P–O–W–E–R, the So-called White Man! But the notes that God makes me write are BLACK, y'dig? The vinyl which eternalises my voice is BLACK also, right? The night into which the sound hangs and vibrates is BLACK! So now I'm working on my new album – 'Pork Is White Meat' – which will reflect this new non-negative situation, vis-à-vis the inter-action of Islam and (white) Western capitalism. Although I will have, per se, a new identity, it is in direct continuity with my pre-fame existence, so that my royalties can keep coming in, which I propose to use to found a Black Muslim Arts Foundation in Nassau. There, black artists will not have to treat with the White Devil. And I can create a positive aura for contemplation and isolation. Unless – and I make one exception – Sting wants me to join his band . . . Chill! "

IKE HITS BACK

Once upon a time, he was the most envied man in the world. A raunchy guitarist who appeared nightly on stage with the Sex Goddess of Soul – Tina Turner – and then went back to his motel room to duet with her some more. His name was Ike – or Mr. Turner to the motel desk clerk. Ike and Tina married young, but fought long and hard. Their relationship was like their most famous recording – on the 'A' side, the thundering joy and passion of 'River Deep, Mountain High'. But on the flip-side, the dark misery of 'Of *Course* the Ikettes Get to Sleep with Me, Tina, That's Why They're Called Ikettes!' Eventually Ike moved on, leaving Tina behind . . . But Tina rebuilt her life and achieved solo stardom in the 80s. For Ike, though, the River ran too fast, and the Mountain proved too high.

Well Def! found him at a run-down, seedy motel in Prattville, Alabama, wearing an old fur coat. He was wearing an old fur coat too, which gave us something to talk about. Ike spoke in a low, rumbling voice like a train in the Southern night. It was so convincing, people arrived in his room carrying luggage and Amtrak tickets. Ike was very understanding – he threw them out. I asked if he was bitter about Tina's success.

❝ Bitter? No, man. I mean, I taught that woman everything she knew. When we argued she had to scream at the top of her voice to get heard – that's how she developed that timber-wolf yell. And when I used to slide into the bed next to her, she learned how to squirm and shake real good so as to put me off. As for the so-called 'Wall of Sound' that Phil Spector was supposed to have invented – Tina and I gave him that, by throwing bottles and pans at each other in our kitchen when we were a fussin'. So a lot of things were kinda taken from me – Tina even took the first letter of my name, because I was born Mike Turner. So, am I bitter? No man. ❞

Next **Well Def!** asked him how he coped with a woman of such outrageous sexuality as Tina.

❝ I didn't like her in all those short skirts, man. Skirts! They were more like pelmets. I thought she looked cheap. But then she hated my tank-top sweaters. She thought *they* looked cheap. She was right – I ripped 'em off from some Navaho Indians who came backstage one night. They were looking to autograph Tina's pelmet. I showed them the door – then the underground car-park and the toilets. The thing that bugged me most was her wigs – she was always wearing wigs, man. Woman wasn't even bald. She cared more about those wigs than me – she eloped with one of 'em for a while, and spent some time up at Niagara Falls. But they fell out – the hairs that is, and she came back to her good old Ike. At least I think it was Tina – cos she'd gotten herself a new Canadian beaver wig. Still wears it from what I see today. We tried to make good again, but when she bad-mouthed my white safari jacket that was the final straw. Said I looked like some dude called Engelbert Humperdinck. I sacked her from the band. Then I saw Engelbert Humperdinck, and sacked my jacket. You know what happened after that – Tina became a superstar; her wigs went on to form *The Muppet Show;* my jacket got a lead part in *Dynasty;* and I went broke. But I'm fighting back, man. I'm going back on the road, with my trusty axe. I've given up the guitar, the axe is better for my image. You see you don't get nowhere being nice! ❞

THE LATEST HIP-HOP CHART

1	**Give Peace a Chance** *(Remix)* Warlord Attila (CIA Records)	**6**	**Register and Vote** Jackmaster Man-With-No-Name (Anonymous)
2	**Stop the Violence - Now** D.J. Mafiosa and The Hitmen (Cosanostra)	**7**	**Just Chill and Be Cool** Retaliation, featuring Dirty Robbie (Revenge)
3	**Ditch Yo Weapon, Sucka** *(12-inch)* Magnum Force (Vigilante)	**8**	**Nuclear Freezion Movement** Bomb the Base (Trident)
4	**Turn Yo Back on Crack** *(Club Remix)* Grandmaster Street Value (Sniff)	**9**	**Save the Planet** Captain Green and the Exxons (US Oceana)
5	**The Poverty Scandal** *(Inner City Nightmare)* L.L. Kruggerand-Chain (Bullion)	**10**	**Respect for Women** *(Extended Version)* Prince Lover S'Xualitee (Equality)

BLUES 'N' SOUL TRIVIA TEST!

Below you'll see some of the all-time great black artists of the past decade.

All you have to do is MATCH the SUPER GROUP to their best known chart-topping hit!

1 The Detroit Spinners

2 The Detroit Bobbinturners

3 The Detroit Carding Shop Operatives

4 The Detroit Lace-Makers' Guild of Employees

5 The Three Degrees

6 The Third Degree

7 The Five BA Honours Degrees (Failed)

8 The Seventeen Open University Degrees Done in Holloway

9 The Isley Brothers

10 The Four Tops

11 The Four Bottoms

12 The Four Skins

13 Smokey Robinson and the Miracles

14 Chesty Robinson and the Acts of God

15 Tubercular Robinson and the Inexplicable Phenomena

16 Gob-it–Up Robinson and the Pools Winners

A Tears of a Clown	**E** Reach Out and I'll Be There	**I** Blame It on the Boogie	**M** Ain't No Mountain High Enough
B Tears of a Ventriloquist	**F** Reach Out and I Won't Be There	**J** Blame It on the Time of the Month	**N** Ain't No Mountie High Enough (Canadian Version)
C Tears of a Quantity Surveyor	**G** Reach Out and I May Be There	**K** Blame It on Edwina Currie	**O** Ain't No Monty High Enough (Second World War Version)
D Tears of a Wet Fish Importer	**H** Reach Out and I'll Be There as Long as I Can Cancel My Dental Appointment	**L** Blame It on the Failure of the England Defence to Pick Up the West German Winger	**P** Two Little Boys

wELL#def:

ROCK STARS AND JESUS

Which of these guys is the Messiah? Answer: they all are, or that's what they want you to believe. The **WELL-HARD NEWSDESK's** researchers have come up with the following strange facts:

Ever since John Lennon said that The Beatles were more popular than Jesus, rock musicians have been trying to go one better by actually becoming holy men. Peter Gabriel's halfway there already! Look at Sting - he used to be a typical star, entertaining the world with his personal thoughts on life, like "Do Do Do Do Da Da Da". So when I heard he was trying to save the rain forests of Brazil, I thought it was just a tax dodge - all the conifer plantations in Scotland must have been bagged by Pink Floyd! He's even started wearing sandals and flowing robes, so kids in wheelchairs can reach out to him on stage, touch the hem of his garment and be healed . . . Whatever happened to 'Don't Stand So Close to Me'? Bono only lets himself be photographed from behind, to give that halo effect, and he's built a recording studio in his farmhouse in Ireland, so he can say "This sound was born in a stable" . . .

Geldof's gigs have become Sermons on the Mount - he's doing cover versions of Golden Greats like "Render unto Caesar that which is Caesar's", calling it "Give Me Your Fokking Money" . . . even Bill Wyman got married in a church; all the other Stones were there and they didn't even throw up in the font - *they're all turning into Jesus!*

Well now the God-Squad are fighting back. When she did her last "Monsters of Charity" world tour with Motorhead, Mother Theresa insisted on a pint of Jack Daniels in her dressing-room and toy-Beastie Boys waiting at every stage door; after gigging Wembley Stadium, Billy Graham climbed into his 12-track stereo coach with selected bimbos from the Mormon Tabernacle Choir and knocked back the holy water spritzers as he watched videos of the dirty bits from *The Last Temptation of Christ*; when chambermaids went to clean up Archbishop Desmond Tutu's hotel room they found it knee-deep in torn-up pages from the Gideon Bible!

The **WELL-HARD NEWSDESK** says: the next time you open the door to two neat and tidy Jehovah's Witnesses trying to sell you *The Watchtower*, check them out - it could be Bros, desperate to get into Rock's Hall of Fame!

WHERE ARE THEY NOW?

– MUNGO JERRY

Remember the man on the left? Go on – course you do. Remember how Andy Warhol once said that Everybody Could Be Famous for Fifteen Minutes . . . you know, *Andy Warhol*. Fair-haired bloke – did a bit of painting? Advertised soup. American. I think. No? Anyway, rock music has its fair share of people who were famous for about fifteen minutes, and who then went back to leading ordinary, boring lives like the rest of us. They were victims of a disease which takes a terrible toll of rock musicians – a disease called nostalgia. You see, if everybody in the business was successful and went on for a long time, there'd be no nostalgia industry. And this geezer on the left was one of the greatest.

His name was Mungo Jerry – easily confused with a popular scouring liquid of the day – who hit Number One in June 1970 with a song called 'In the Summertime'. The record was, in fact, due for release in January, until a whiz-kid in marketing hit on June as a better alternative. For a few wild, crazy weeks Mungo Jerry was the hottest act around. People just loved the chugging rhythm of the record and the unusual sound created by band member Dave 'Cheeks' Wiggins blowing into a jug. Actually we've made that name up because not even professors of nostalgia remember who the bloke with his head in an empty cider flagon was. The same man, however, is credited with creating the sound effects of the car starting up and driving off at the end of the record – well, all that blowing had to have some effect on his bum.

The critics coined the term 'jug music' for the record, and for a few weeks it seemed likely to be *the* sound of the seventies – Frank Sinatra was said to be recording a jug album; Keith Richards of The Rolling Stones started sniffing out of jugs; and Rod Stewart experimented by making love to several earthenware pots in Habitat on the King's Road. But then the musicians realised that they were supposed to be getting into *'drugs'*, not 'jugs', and the new sound disappeared into that great catacomb called nostalgia. Mungo Jerry quickly became forgotten and their catchphrase 'sex and jugs and rock 'n' roll' died with them.

This is my mother and father. The one on the left is my mother, the one on the right is my father. They never got married; maybe it was something to do with the fact that my father was already married to someone else. But I know they loved each other because whenever they had an argument, my mother always went with my father to the hospital and waited till they stitched him up.

This is me when I was one year old. I remember being born: one minute I was lying there thinking about rearranging the living-room, the next minute I was being strangled by my umbilical cord. The doctor untangled me, held me upside down and smacked my backside. It wasn't even my fault. And now, whenever I see an extension cable, I have a lot of difficulty breathing.

This is my old school. There was only three people in the class: the teacher, me and a mouse. And that's not much fun you know, especially if the mouse is cleverer than you. If I hadn't trodden on it at playtime, it might have become Prime Minister.

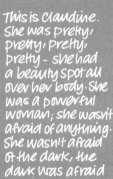

This is Claudine. She was pretty, pretty, pretty, pretty - she had a beauty spot all over her body. She was a powerful woman; she wasn't afraid of anything. She wasn't afraid of the dark, the dark was afraid of her. Whenever she walked into a room, all the lights came on. I fell deeply in love with her; I fell so deeply, they had to send a rescue team to get me back up. I courted her for years but she didn't want to know. I gave her flowers, presents, tried to make her jealous, went out with another woman, gave her three kids. That worked. In the end I married her because she said yes; and pretty soon, everything was coming up roses; we'd planted daffodils but you can't argue with nature.

This is me arriving at Southampton docks. You can't see me in the photograph because I was in my cabin asleep; I didn't wake up for another ten hours and by then we were on our way back to Jamaica. I eventually got here six weeks later suffering from ship-lag.

People told me the only way to get a job in England was with the old school tie. So I wore my old school tie for three years and nothing happened. Then I realised something; not many people in England went to the St. Anne Presbyterian School, Kingston. When I got to England, I never dreamed that I'd ever have a high paid job; and my dream came true – I didn't.

Claudine came over in this boat with the kids. I don't know whose kids they were, but they called me Uncle Deakus, so I guess that was alright.

This is me and Claudine at home. I'm behind the camera. A pity we're not both in the picture together, because she left me soon after that. Ran off with a double-glazing salesman. Sometimes it gets so cold in my flat I wish I'd run off with him myself.

This is when I went to look for a job. I asked this man to take a photo of me looking, but he took my camera instead and made off with it. I caught him and gave him a beating, then took his picture to show my grandchildren that Deakus used to have real vim. I wonder what happened to it. Wonder what happened to my grandchildren.

This was the first job I got – polishing steam engines. After two years I got promoted and they let me do it when the train was standing still. By the time this picture was taken, I'd already fallen off.

I'm an old man now. I can tell I'm getting old because my skin doesn't fit me any more. My blood used to run round my body, now it just hangs around my stomach waiting for the next cup of tea. When you get old, you appreciate that England has things that you don't get in Jamaica – like hypothermia. But you can keep that. There's only one good thing to be said for the cold. Cold Guinness. Cheers!

THE ORIGIN OF CARIBBEAN PLACE NAMES

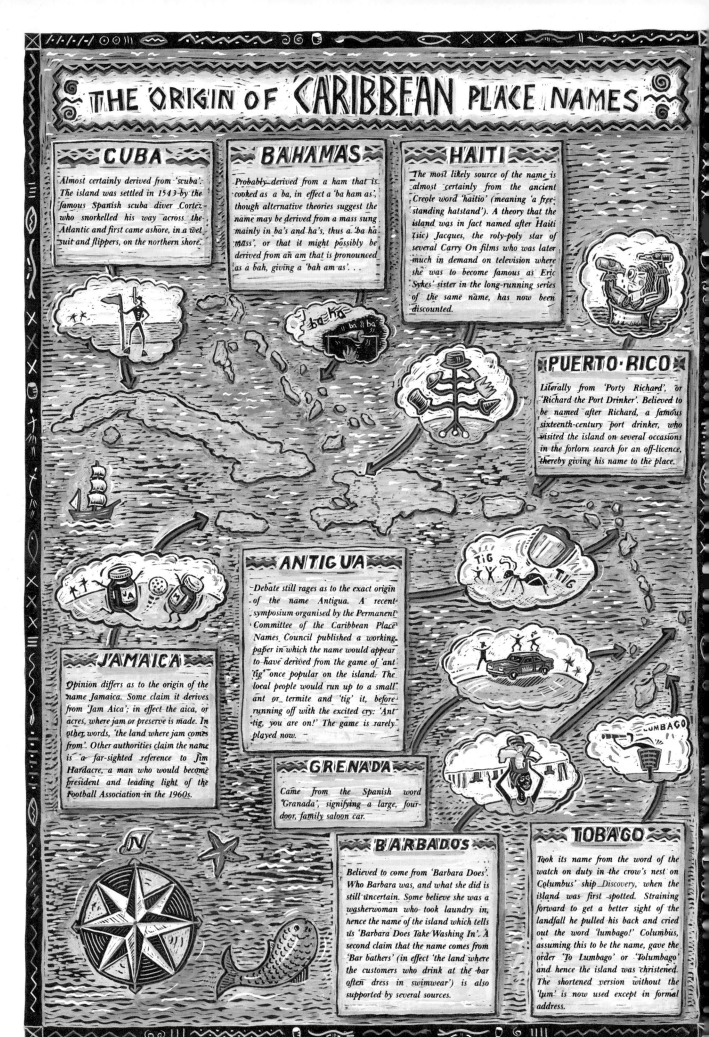

CUBA

Almost certainly derived from 'scuba'. The island was settled in 1543 by the famous Spanish scuba diver Cortez who snorkelled his way across the Atlantic and first came ashore, in a wet suit and flippers, on the northern shore.

BAHAMAS

Probably derived from a ham that is cooked as a ba, in effect a 'ba ham as', though alternative theories suggest the name may be derived from a mass sung mainly in ba's and ha's, thus a 'ba ha mass', or that it might possibly be derived from an am that is pronounced as a bah, giving a 'bah am as'...

HAITI

The most likely source of the name is almost certainly from the ancient Creole word 'haitio' (meaning 'a free-standing hatstand'). A theory that the island was in fact named after Haiti (sic) Jacques, the roly-poly star of several Carry On films who was later much in demand on television where she was to become famous as Eric Sykes' sister in the long-running series of the same name, has now been discounted.

PUERTO·RICO

Literally from 'Porty Richard', or 'Richard the Port Drinker'. Believed to be named after Richard, a famous sixteenth-century port drinker, who visited the island on several occasions in the forlorn search for an off-licence, thereby giving his name to the place.

ANTIGUA

Debate still rages as to the exact origin of the name Antigua. A recent symposium organised by the Permanent Committee of the Caribbean Place Names Council published a working paper in which the name would appear to have derived from the game of 'ant tig' once popular on the island. The local people would run up to a small ant or termite and 'tig' it, before running off with the excited cry: 'Ant-tig, you are on!' The game is rarely played now.

JAMAICA

Opinion differs as to the origin of the name Jamaica. Some claim it derives from 'Jam Aica'; in effect the aica, or acres, where jam or preserve is made. In other words, 'the land where jam comes from'. Other authorities claim the name is a far-sighted reference to Jim Hardacre, a man who would become president and leading light of the Football Association in the 1960s.

GRENADA

Came from the Spanish word 'Granada', signifying a large, four-door, family saloon car.

BARBADOS

Believed to come from 'Barbara Does'. Who Barbara was, and what she did is still uncertain. Some believe she was a washerwoman who took laundry in, hence the name of the island which tells us 'Barbara Does Take Washing In'. A second claim that the name comes from 'Bar bathers' (in effect 'the land where the customers who drink at the bar often dress in swimwear') is also supported by several sources.

TOBAGO

Took its name from the word of the watch on duty in the crow's nest on Columbus' ship Discovery, when the island was first spotted. Straining forward to get a better sight of the landfall he pulled his back and cried out the word 'lumbago!' Columbus, assuming this to be the name, gave the order 'To Lumbago' or 'Tolumbago' and hence the island was christened. The shortened version without the 'lum' is now used except in formal address.

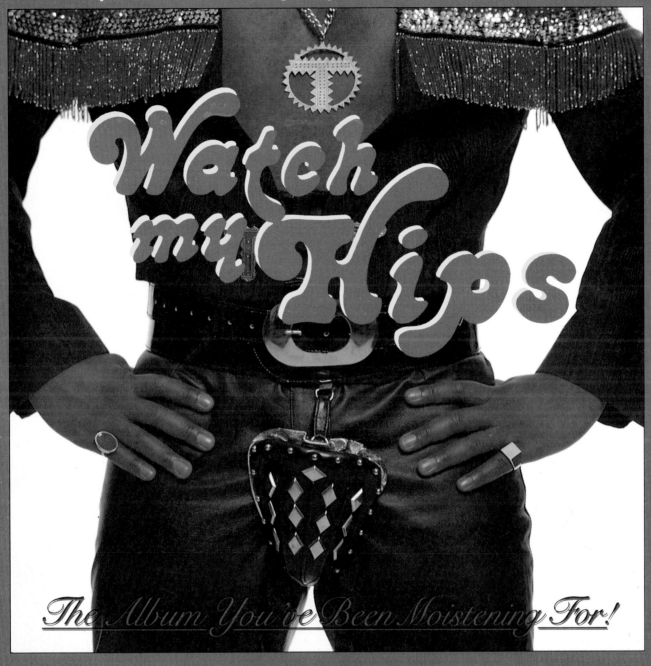
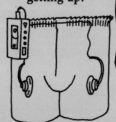

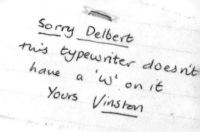

Sorry Delbert
this typewriter doesn't
have a 'W' on it
Yours Vinston

HOME OFFICE
Queen Anne's Gate London SW1H 9AT

APPLICATION FOR COMMUNITY RADIO LICENCE

NAME

DELBERT VILKINS

~~AGE~~ None of your business. Let's just say
Vhitney Houston still finds me totally
irresistible

~~ADDRESS~~

Do you think I'm stupid?
I'm not gonna get raided again!

PREVIOUS BROADCASTING EXPERIENCE

Are you deaf? Everybody in London heard the Brixton Broadcasting
Corporation and Crucial FM. Both totally vicked,guy! Turntables so
big British Rail hired them to reverse their engines on! Ginormous
speakers I let homeless families live in during the day!! It vas
so loud kids in Australia rang up to complain - "Cripes,Delbert -
I'm trying to revise!"!!!

WHEN DID YOU LEAVE YOUR PREVIOUS EMPLOYMENT?

As soon as I heard the gooks from the Department of Trade and
Industry breaking down my front door with an axe! I said I didn't
realise I'd been breaking the lav - I thought DTI vas a stereo
shop in Tottenham Court Road,Disco Turntables Incorporated!

TYPE OF EQUIPMENT

scale model - one hundredth
actual size

"hydro-electric energy source
- the sound I make is <u>ecologically</u> sound,guys!"

WHAT DO YOU CONSIDER TO BE THE MAIN FUNCTION OF COMMUNITY RADIO?

Another dumb question - let me spell it out for you pinheads! To bring Delbert Vilkins to the masses, playing the most crucial music in creation! I mean, the kids are sick of hearing about those ancient geezers on Radio 1 enjoying a nice cup of coffee and the movies they've seen that the rest of us don't get for six months! They vant to hear ME enjoying a nice can of Red Stripe and talking about the pirate video of 'Nightmare on Elm Street 28' that Vinston's just got hold of for me - before they've even made numbers 24 to 27!

HAVE YOU EVER APPLIED FOR ANY OTHER BROADCASTING POSTS?

Of course I have! Director-General of the BBC (that's the other BBC, the impostor)...Head of Sky-TV - they never even replied to my reverse-charge fax, just ripped off my programming ideas (loads of classic old progs like The Love Boat and Sale of the Century)...I even tried to buy Bush House ("Today Crucial FM, Tomorrov the Vorld Service!") but my mortgage application vas turned down. It's a major conspiracy, guys, to keep me from my public!

GIVE DETAILS OF FINANCIAL BACKING, ADVERTISING, SPONSORS, OTHER SOURCES OF INCOME, ETC.

I operate a barter system, right? If it's lunchtime and there's nothing in the fridge except my socks, chilling out, I do a quick ad for Marks and Spencers and before you can say "Chicken Tikka" outside the flat there's a box full of triple-decker sarnies, dips, Belgian chocs...they tried sending clothes once, but I made Vinston take 'em back and keep the refunded dosh as his salary! And here's a message for the Serious Shoe Shop, Kennington Road - I'm about to put you on the map, guys, so I expect you to put me on the mailing list for freebies!

GIVE A SAMPLE OF YOUR TYPICAL OUTPUT

~~Classical~~
~~Opera~~
~~Light Orchestral~~
~~Middle of the Road~~
~~Pop~~

Other (please specify)

Beastie Boys
Funkadelic
Al Green
Prince
Aretha Franklin
Jam & Levis
Cookie Crev
Prince
De La Soul
Doug E Fresh and the Get Fresh Crev
Neneh Cherry
Adeva
Public Enemy
Vee Papa Girls
Kool Moe Dee
More Prince

NO

PASS TO ROOM 214 FOR DEPORTATION

"Don't vorry about needle-time guys - my roadie gets all the nevest tunes sent via DHL direct from the studios and they're remixed before they even. knov they've been nicked! KNOV VHAT I MEAN?

THE JOHN DUCK FILE

His Name is **John Duck!**
He is a **Dangerous** Man to Know, or to Snicker at When You Hear His Name!
He has **Killed FOURTEEN** People, including Mafia Hit Men, Harlem Drugs Barons, and a Subway Trumpet Busker who Hit a Flat Note which Sounded Like a Snicker!
Yet this Man John Duck **Walks Free!** Because he is **A COP ! ! !**

Here He Tells 'Crime U.S.A.' How He Started Out on His Murderous Road ! !

"My name is John Duck . . . did you snicker just then, asshole? . . . okay, but next time use a Kleenex . . . I was born on the mean side of The Bronx. It doesn't have any other, only mean . . . when the cops shot anyone they used to come round afterwards and take the bullets back. I liked their style – they recycled *before* it became fashionable. The kids on our block grew up fast. Real fast. By the time I was six, I was eleven. When I was eleven, I was twenty. And by the time I was twenty, I just managed to avoid cremation. It was a tough neighborhood. The whites hated the blacks, the blacks hated the Mexicans, the Mexicans hated the Chinese, and everyone hated the Romanians, even though we didn't have no Romanians in the neighborhood. You ain't Romanian, by any chance?"

*In 1976, Duck's **entire family** were innocent victims of a Triad-Mafia shoot-out in a New York Chinese Restaurant. Duck only managed to escape the **fire-storm** by wrapping himself in pancakes and smearing himself with plum sauce. From that moment on, he dedicated his life to cleaning up the city . . . starting with the Chinese restaurant.*

"I work on the NYPD's 'SFAQL' Squad – short for 'Shoot First Ask Questions Later'. I never knew why it was called that – every time I asked, somebody shot at me. I was first assigned to the 96th Precinct, which was run by the Romanians. I cleared them out with silver bullets, garlic grenades and a threat to install parliamentary democracy. Then the Sicilians moved in . . . led by a guy known only as The Sicilian. That made him hard to spot. I'd kick down the doors of dope-dens and ask if The Sicilian was in there – 56 guys would stand up and start shooting at me. I got tired of asking questions . . ."

*After several months on the case, Duck turned up evidence linking The Sicilian with his family's **massacre** – a Mafia training video entitled 'How to Do a Runner from a Chinese Restaurant'. This was later dubbed from the original Sicilian and released as a feature by Michael Winner. Meanwhile, Duck received a **tip-off** regarding The Sicilian's real name – Al Dente . . it was to prove the vital clue!*

"I spent nights prowling the streets looking for Signor Dente. I had two Magnum 45s strapped to my belt, together with an Uzi machine gun, ten stun grenades, a flame-thrower, a ten-inch field gun, and a Swiss Army knife. I didn't get any trouble, apart from my pants falling down. Then one Tuesday I finally caught him coming out of a downtown disco he owned – Dente's Inferno. I let him have everything I'd got on my belt. Twelve slugs from the Magnums, thirty-eight rounds from the Uzi, ten cubic feet of CS gas, a ten-inch shell, a jet of burning oil, and a little metal spike for getting the stones out of horses' hooves. I asked him if he knew the name Duck. He snickered – so I got real mad. When the medics turned up, they thought he was confetti. I booked him on several litter violations, bleeding on metropolitan property, etc. I went home, had a few beers and showered. I was tired. Tired of crime. Tired of being a Psycho Cop. But I knew the city was a safer place. I slept well that night."

John Duck was later stripped of his badge by New York Police, but was allowed to keep his belt. He left America for England, where he now works as a Community Liaison Officer for the Metropolitan Police.

They Came From Somewhere Else

CONFERENCE CENTRES

This is the **WELL-HARD NEWSDESK** bringing you a special undercover report on a growing menace to the fabric of our country. They call themselves "Conference Hotels", but I'm here to warn you that they are in fact Giant Propagators planted by an alien life-force bent on repopulating the earth with **GREYMEN!**

Here are some of the tell-tale signs that let you know you are in the presence of a **GREYMAN**. The *Lapel-Badge,* that identifies them to each other and distinguishes them from real people. They camouflage themselves with interchangeable names: "Derek Barry" . . . "Barry John" . . . "John Derek". The *Radio-Pager* strapped to the belt that keeps them in touch with the Mother-Ship hovering above the earth and relays urgent messages like "Human being standing at bar. Go and bore to death with stories about sales targets and differentials". The *Cordless Phone,* a symbol of their importance, which they use to contact each other as the final moments of take-over approach. Their lips are saying "Yeah, I've got a window at 10.30 on Friday", but their minds are thinking "I would like to Pod with this Earth-Woman".

To find out more, I infiltrated one of these so-called Conference Hotels, and these are the facts. As you enter you are handed a "Welcome Pack", the first attempt to destroy your mind. It contains Greying Devices designed to turn you into one of Them, like a cloth impregnated with after-shave that they try and convince you will clean your shoes. I had no truck with it, so put my shoes outside in the corridor. I saw nobody, but when I went back into the room the sheets on the bed had been turned down and there was a chocolate mint on the pillow. Is that weird shit or what? I went to the bathroom to dispose of the mint. As I switched on the light there was a hum as a hidden extractor tried to suck out my vital juices ready for body-transference. The end of the toilet-roll was folded into a symbolic "V". I turned on the television: every channel showed scenes of advanced Podding. In a panic, I tried to escape but the windows were sealed. I ran down to the bar. A group of **GREYMEN** were still talking about their company cars, even though it was three o'clock in the morning and they *weren't drunk!* Next day, even though only one hundred of them had checked in, two hundred **GREYMEN** came down to breakfast. They had replicated overnight. They all got up from the table at the same time and using the same coded language – "This isn't getting the baby washed" . . . what baby? The Demon Seed must have been sown! – all went into a room with a blackboard and an overhead projector to plan their campaign of World Domination . . .

This is a typical "Conference Hotel". Who built it? Nobody knows. They appear overnight on the outskirts of large cities, biding their time. So you have been warned. They're coming. If you see one of them near you, and hear the sound of the theme from *The Deer Hunter* being played by a lift . . . **MOVE!**

JACK-IN-THE-BOX

Down and out in London. A Special Independent Report

"My name is Jack. Originally, I come from Liverpool. Well, not *originally*, because that would have to be Africa. I had a nice place in Toxteth, but the police gave it a thorough search during the riots. They found what they wanted – a black man having a quiet nap on a couch. I was arrested and charged with possession of a house. After that I came to London to look for work, but Michael Heseltine had been sent up to Liverpool to create jobs. I've always had great timing – in the sixties it was fashionable not to do work or to have property. Here's me doing it in the eighties.

"I can't remember my surname, which is just as well as I'd have to pay poll tax on it. I mean the rates on this box were bad enough, cos as you can see it's got a conservatory and open fireplace. But because I live by the river, I was being crucified. Of course I've still got my country pad – a none-up, one-down fertiliser bag in Green Park, but I don't think I'll hang onto it. There's an awful lot of Townies moving in, sacked merchant bankers and such. I suppose I'm what you'd call a NIMBY – Not–In–My–Bag–You!

"I like to start my day with a good wash and brush-up. These new stainless steel karzis are just the job. They clean themselves every time they're used, so when someone comes out, I can nip in before the door shuts and get a free shower. Failing that, there's a good carwash on the Waterloo Road – I can walk through on the blind side of the driver, or lie face-up on the roof-rack, open my mouth and get a good teeth clean too.

"Being into a healthy life-style, I like a good hearty breakfast. So I go down to the big extractor fan at the Savoy Kitchens, where ten good sniffs will keep me going all morning. At lunchtime I usually pick up a potato in the gutter down Berwick Street market. I bake it inside a Belisha beacon cos I don't trust those microwaves. For dinner, I stick to just half a Big Mac in Oxford Street – the half that people can't face and throw away. The company puts bins outside specially so I know where to look – that's what I call fast food.

"I like to exercise so I've designed my own aerobics programme. For my back I do a lot of bending forward – to throw up (see 'diet', above). I work my legs on the London Underground running up and down all the broken escalators. (I pay for my ticket with tips from grateful passengers after I've pushed buskers onto the live rail.) And I keep my biceps in shape, by opening the door for confused cashpoint customers who can't get in with their card. And if I fancy a break from my box, I can sleep in here – my 'Crashpoint' I call it.

"I make my own entertainment – by sticking together left over bits of film from Wardour Street bins. My pal The Judge (he's always asleep on his bench) acts as projectionist because he's got a torch. Sometimes we get lucky and see all the censored bits from hot films like 'Nightmare on Elm Street 8 – Freddy Loses His Temper'. But on the downside, we see a lot before they've added the special effects – 'Who Framed Roger?' and 'Close Encounters of the First Kind'. I'm also a bit of a theatre-goer – ten minutes before the final curtain when the staff go home usually. I hate 'whodunnits' because I never know 'whatsbindunn' in the first place. Occasionally, I take out my girlfriend. She's a bag-lady – plastic of course. We don't have plans to shack up yet as we value our independence. Besides, we haven't got a shack. Some nights I go over to her place, other nights she brings her place over to mine.

"I tend to avoid the centre of London when I'm looking for clothes. Hampstead and Islington are the places to find good gear, because the people are so image-conscious, they'd rather throw clothes out than be seen taking them to Oxfam. Anytime I see a TV documentary about seal-clubbing in the window of Curry's, I leg it up here, because I know I'm onto a good thing. So I'm a supporter of Green Politics – but then again, the destruction of the ozone layer has brought me a couple of mild winters, and a steady supply of redundant ski-wear.

"Because of the coat, I get a bit of flak from Animal Rights activists but, on the other hand, when it's cold or raining it gets me into the House of Lords, where they think I'm the Lord Chancellor after an all-night sitting. This means I have to vote with the Tories, but I'd do that any-

way if I had a vote of my own. I've got a lot to thank them for. Ten years ago I had a good job, a mortgage, and money in the bank. Now I haven't got a care in the world and my money's in an off-shore account – the Trafalgar Square fountains.

"Yes, life's been pretty good to me. But if there's one thing that makes me see red – apart from being followed round by photographers from the *Independent Magazine* – it's spongers! You come home after a hard day's work and find people taking advantage of you! I say to them 'Haven't you got homes to go to?' and they say 'No!' What kind of an answer is that? I'm sorry but these squatters have got to learn to stand on their own two feet, not sleep next to mine! Why can't they follow my example – I got on my bike; I did it my way; I rejoiced, rejoiced; I didn't drool and drivel about caring; I always knew there was no such thing as society. And here I am: Jack–in–the–Box. A true success story of the 1980s!"

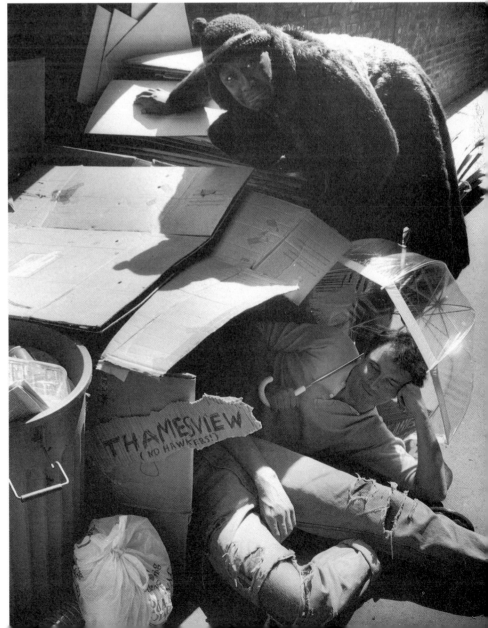

Meet my car, guys – a customised 1963 stretch Ford Zodiac, courtesy of Winston/NASA/Lego/ Eat–Your–Heart–Out–James– Bond Productions!

INSET OF DASHBOARD:

(1) HANDS-FREE CAR-PHONE (2) HANDS-FREE STEERING WHEEL (3) POLICE RADAR DETECTOR (so powerful it detects French police as well) (4) INDICATOR SYNCHRONISER SWITCH (links hazard warning lights to stereo, providing public with free disco) (5) SPEEDOMETER (graded in Warps) (6) IONISER (for laid-back atmosphere) (7) CHROMISER (in case of chrome shortage) (8) IN-CAR MIDI SYSTEM (CD and Video-CD player included) (9) "REVENGER" DEFENCE SYSTEM (Death Ray/Front-Mounted Machine Gun/Grenade Launcher – motorists think it's a Yuppie toy. It's not) (10) "COBRA" ALARM SYSTEM

INTERIOR DETAILS

(1) COMPARTMENT FOR RING-PULL INFLATABLE WHITNEY HOUSTON (for attending film premières, etc.) (2) COCKTAIL BAR & BARMAN (will also sell drinks to public at red lights) (3) MICROWAVE OVEN LINKED TO SATELLITE SYSTEM (beams in food direct from Jamaica) (4) 24-TRACK RECORDING STUDIOS (in case I feel a song coming on) (5) KEITH PROWSE TICKET BOOTH (for concerts, shows etc.) (6) CAR SWEETS DISPENSER (car occasionally reaches such high speeds that ears must be "popped") (7) 72-inch TV/VIDEO SCREEN (for in-flight movies) (8) GUCCI SEAT-BELTS (for restraint *and* style) (9) ROOF-MOUNTED SHOWER-UNIT AND HAIR-DRYER (my body is on 24-hour alert) (10) TWO FLUFFY POLICEMEN'S HELMETS (hang in rear window to annoy plods)

BLACK CAB (no room for chauffeur, girlfriend or baby in car)

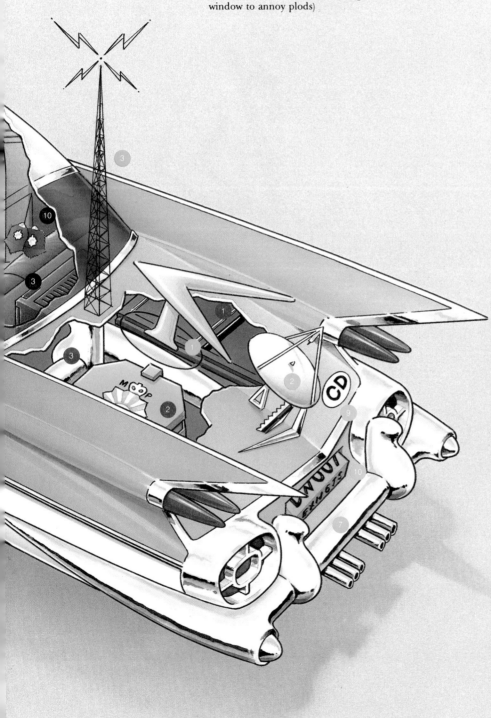

CUTAWAY OF BOOT:

1) TROUSER PRESS (2) IMITATION WHEEL CLAMP (3) SPARE CHROME

EXTERIOR DETAILS

(1) TV AERIAL (for broadcasting from the car on the "Delbert Wilkins Lifestyle Channel") (2) SATELLITE DISH (inverted, to repel signals from Rupert Murdoch) (3) RADIO MAST (for jamming of "Radio One Roadshow") (4) WHITEWALL TYRES (ecologically re-cycled from two million unsold packets of Richard Branson's "Mates" - for extra grip in the wet, know what I mean?) (5) TITANIUM HUB-CAPS (ragamuffin proof, linked to "Cobra" alarm system - see dashboard telemetry) (6) HIGH-PROFILE TINTED WINDOWS (coated on inside only, so I can't see out, but everyone can see me!) (7) CHROME TRIM, EXHAUST PIPE AND BUMPERS (in case I need to see my reflection outside the car) (8) LASER-GUIDED HEADLIGHTS (dipped...in chrome!) (9) CD PLATE (tells public I have a Compact Disc player on board) (10) BABYLON-PROOF NUMBERPLATES (revolve every 30 seconds to confuse police computer)

WELL-HARD NEWS FLASH

What People Really Say On The Car Phone

Ever wondered what those people using car-phones are actually saying? An exclusive "Well-Hard" phone-tap can now reveal what a guy like this is doing with his Hands-Free Facility!

Hello? Hello Deirdre! Look, can you tell the boss I'll be about half-an-hour late. I'm stuck in the most awful traffic jam!

Hello? Hello Tom! Just calling to say hello really. Yes, that's right, it is traffic noise in the background! Just got a car-phone, see!

Hello? Hello – look I've been trying for a line for 20 minutes now, and I keep being disconnected. Hello? Shit!

Hello? Hello Tom – me again! Sorry to bother you, but there's this rather dishy bird in a convertible GTi next to me in the jam, and I just wanted to sort of impress her, you know?

Hello? Hello, who's that? Where? Oh, sorry, wrong number! Er, je m'excuse, c'est un numero en erreur, je crois! Pardon!

Hello? Yes, hello Gary. That's right – I'm a regular car-phone patroller for your show! Well, Gary, I'm just approaching the M25 intersection, and there's a tailback of about three miles, so don't make the mistake I did, and avoid that area if you can. Cheers, Gary!

Hello? Hello Deirdre – me again! Look, sorry – but I'm going to be an *hour* late now! The bloody traffic's getting worse. Still haven't got past the M25 yet! Give him my apologies will you. I'll do my best to be there by eleven.

Hello? Yes, good morning to you too, Brian! I'm a first-time caller, yes, but I just wanted to say that I think it's about time something was done about the country's traffic problems! I mean, they're stifling industry and commerce . . . Hello? Sorry, Brian, I'm breaking up . . . Damn!

Hello? Hello Deirdre – look I can't make it in till after lunchtime now! Bloody police have arrested me for dangerous driving! I mean, did you know it was an offence to drive on the hard shoulder while using a car-phone, cos I bloody didn't!

Hello? Hello, darling – look there's not much doing at the office apparently, so I'm heading back home now! See you in about an hour. Er, better make that two darling – just running into a bit of a jam, I'm afraid!

Delbert Wilkins
GUIDES to
CRUCIALITY

Okay Cruciality – come and sit on my knee, man . . . What are you doing? Get off! I meant my metaphorical knee, not the one that's wearing a silk Versace pantaloon! I want to talk about your education, right? Cos you're two now and should be starting to think about University. Well, I've got some bad news for you – the Government's fitted every school and college in the country with turnstiles, so you've got to pay to get in! And all you come out with is a free clipboard and ballpoint-pen and an overdraft on your student loan bigger than Bernard Manning's toilet seat! And anyway, the whole system's been messed up by this Kenneth Baker who thinks he's a bit of a dude cos he grooms himself with Brylcreem. Talk about wrong-headed! That's the stuff they used to grease slipways with to launch ships . . . and that's what gave us North Sea Oil! See? That's a bit of history I've taught you there . . . you got it Croosh – I'm opting you out. You don't need no core curriculum cos you're going to be privately educated – by me!

Forget the three R's man – I'm giving you four. *RAGAMUFFINRY* is what my Dad Sonny instilled into the infant Delbert and made me the Big Sooper-Dooper you see chilling before you today. Like how to play wicked dominoes in backrooms with no light and still be able to see the white spots! *RUDENESS* is not what you say to a policeman when he stops you in the street for not having insurance or a tax-disc – and that's just when you're walking, man! – that comes under the heading of *RUN!* Rudeness is what you say to a lady. Like, when I first met your mum I complimented her on the way she looked . . . at me! I said, "Hey girl – would you like me to let you take me out?" She said yes. Actually when she worked it out, what she meant to say was "No" – but it was too late: you were already a twinkle in my Ray-Bans! And the fourth R, which deals with anything you might not know, is *RING WINSTON*. In fact there's a fifth – *REVERSE THE CHARGES!*

So, let me finish by teaching you a little poem, guy, to carry with you through life. It's by that Kipling geezer, whose poetry is nearly as good as his cakes:

If you can keep your head together while all about you are losing their hair and their sponditiousness . . .
If you can meet with triumph and disaster you shouldn't be driving a clapped-out British sports car . . .
If you can talk with crowds and keep your virtue . . . you must be wearing the wrong suit, guy!
If you can fill the unforgiving minute with a three-hour rap from Public Enemy . . .
. . . Yours is the earth, and everything that's in it . . . and – which is more – you'll be a better and more crucial man than I am, Gunga Din, my son!!

CHARLIE CHEDDAR
The Forgotten Music Hall Star

Ask any of the legendary stars from the turn of the century to name the comedian who was the biggest influence on their career, and you wouldn't get an answer, because they're all dead. But if they could still speak, without exception they'd reply 'Charlie Cheddar'. Charlie was born of an English mother and a West Indian sailor she met at Bristol Docks who later disappeared to sea. The man's surname escaped her too and she called Charlie after the place he was conceived: the Cheddar Gorge. In fact, his first name was Charlie Gorge but, typical of him, he foresaw that there might one day be an Arsenal footballer called 'Charlie George' and thoughtfully changed it to prevent confusion. Charlie Chester, whose real name was Charlie Nicholas, later did the same thing – just one of many comedians who 'borrowed' Charlie's ideas.

However, the change of name was to stand Charlie in good stead. He ran away at the age of seven to join a travelling circus and was billed as 'Charlie Cheddar the Human Cheese Football', when he was shot every evening out of a howitzer field gun, landed up to 25 miles away and had to walk back in time for the matinée. Sometimes he would load the gun up with double the amount of powder so he could drop in on his mother who was in the workhouse. One day he took his washing with him, was late back after waiting for it to dry and 'got fired for the third time that day', as he put it in later years, when asked why he decided to concentrate on visual rather than verbal comedy.

Dressed only in the burnt rags he stood up in, he joined Fred Karno's troupe and his tramp-like appearance impressed the young Charlie Chaplin (whose real name was Charlie Williams) to a considerable degree. Chaplin soon developed a routine called 'Hit the Black Guy' but, after six months and six fractured skulls, Charlie Cheddar came up with a variation, 'Hit the Black Guy, But Not So Hard'. This wasn't as popular with audiences, and even less successful was 'Don't Hit the Black Guy at All'. Chaplin lost interest in the double-act and, even though Charlie desperately wrote a new sketch called 'Okay, You Can Hit the Black Guy If You Want to', Karno had run out of patience and Charlie was forced to set out for America to try and make his fortune in the fledgeling film industry. Having no money for the fare he stowed away on a tramp steamer, passing unnoticed among all the other tramps, and landed six hours later on the Isle of Wight.

By the time he realised his mistake he had founded the Cowes Film Industry and made some 50 films which were shown all over the Ryde Odeon. These included such silent classics as 'The Four Donkeymen of the Apocalypse', 'Ben Herd', 'A Countess from Shanklin' and 'Birth of a Station' this last containing the famous scene in which, while waiting for a train on a platform with only a broken cigarette machine for company, Charlie gets so frustrated that he rolls up his sock and smokes it. This idea was stolen by Chaplin when he ate his boot in 'The Gold Rush'. Hearing of this, Charlie left the Isle of Wight in a rage for Hollywood, only to find when he got there that Charlie Chaplin was also using the tramp costume, the burnt-feet painful walk, the moustache – but had substituted a cane for Charlie's famous inflatable giraffe to prevent a lawsuit.

Charlie was devastated and, in desperation, went back to some of his old routines, but had forgotten how much gunpowder to put in the gun, with near-fatal results. A spectator at one of these fiascos was Harold Lloyd, and Charlie's predicament was the making of Lloyd's career. Charlie was even reduced to reviving 'Hit the Black Guy', and his suffering in the name of art was the inspiration behind Stan Laurel and Ben Turpin, who shamelessly exploited Charlie's physical discomfort.

He had one last stab at fame – the Ultimate Gag, where a house would fall on him, leaving him standing among its ruins surrounded by the open window-frame. But as he was standing there waiting for the cameras to turn, Charlie Chaplin happened to pass by and thought it would be funnier with the window shut. He was wrong, and showed Buster Keaton the correct way to do it, but it was too late: Charlie Cheddar was not only dead, but buried.

Hello. Remember me?

[T]he funny black guy with the big hat. You know who I am, don't you? [It's] on the tip of your tongue, isn't it? [Yo]u know the face but you can't [re]member the name.

[W]ell I can remember it: Algernon [ ] Winston Spencer Churchill [Disr]aeli Pitt the Younger Pitt the Elder [etc.] Razzamataz. I was with Lenny [Hen]ry back in the seventies on *Tiswas*; I [wa]s one of his characters. We went [eve]rywhere together. I was a star – [eve]rybody knew me. I had [a] catchphrase; you remember the [cat]chphrase, don't you: OOOOOOOO-OOOOKAAAAAAAAAAAY. That was [a h]ousehold word – never mind what [ho]usehold – take my word for it: OO-[OO]OOOOOKAAAAAAAAAY. Every-[on]e was saying it: shopkeepers, traffic [war]dens, solicitors, checkout girls, [pol]iticians, the Royal Family. Doctors [wo]uld say to their patients: "Open your [mo]uth and say, OOOOOOO-OOOOOOKAAAAAAAAAAY." Never [mi]nd Loadsamoney – I was there first.

[A]nd remember the bread and [con]densed milk sandwiches? I [us]ed to eat those all the time; they [ma]de me ill but I still did it because [tha]t's what Lenny wanted me to do. I'd [say] to him: "I'm a Rastaman, why [sho]uld I eat bread and condensed milk [san]dwiches? Why can't I eat something [nor]mal like beef and onion pie?" He'd [say]: "Because it's not so funny. Bread [and] condensed milk sandwiches are [fun]ny; you have to eat those." So I'd [say] "Alright, Lenny, I will, because I'm a [pro]fessional."

[T]hat was then, in the old days, when [ ] he needed me. But things changed [afte]r that; he started seeing me as a [ste]reotyped character. Me! I couldn't [bel]ieve it! He said I was over the top, [that] the Rasta hat was too much, and [OO]OOKAAAY was cartoony and he [wa]nted to develop other characters [wit]h more depth and realism – where [did] he pick those words up? Not from [me.] But he was the boss, and so I didn't [min]d when he stopped doing me.

[I] decided to take a well-earned break [an]d see the world. The Betty Ford [Cli]nic was great. They really looked [aft]er me and helped me kick the habit. [The] cold turkey was tough at first, but I [soo]n got used to the taste and didn't [mi]ss the condensed milk at all. And [afte]r all the Phantom Phlan Phlinging – [eve]n though you tried to get out of the [wa]y, you'd always end up swallowing [son]e of it – the hash brownies were a [rea]l treat!

[A]nyway, I'm back now. I got my P45 [ ] and my reference from Lenny: "*If [you] want a geezer in a funny hat for the [Sta]te-Opening-of-Parliament gig, check [out] Algernon. He's under 'OOOKAAAY' in [the] Yellow Pages.*" But here's a message [for] Delbert and all the others – one of [the]se days you'll say "Know what I [me]an?" and Lenny'll say "No – and I [don]'t care, either." Your crucial days [are] numbered, man!

No chance of that with me around, readers. Katanga!! (Brilliant catch-phrase, eh?!)

Only a couple of pages to wait for sexy and violent, undercover rompings as the crow flies! Don't be so disgusting Ziggy!

JOIN ME!

AT THE BRITISH RAIL GUARDS' CHARM SCHOOL!

"I DON'T MAKE THE RULES, MATE!"

Your train has broken down halfway between Coventry and Nuneaton. It's the middle of winter and there's no heating or buffet. After an hour and a half you are grabbed by an irate First-Class passenger who says he's late for an important business meeting and he's going to kill you.
DO YOU : Kick him off the train and make him walk up the electrified rail to the nearest station to find a fuse?

WRONG!

OR: Ask to see his ticket, tell him he shouldn't be travelling on this train because it's an Orange Saver (Pensioners with Dogs Travelling in Threes) Day, take his name and address, humiliate him in front of the other passengers and offer first aid when he has a heart attack?

RIGHT!

How to be abuser-friendly with difficult customers is one of the many skills we'll teach you at the British Rail Guards' Charm School. Worried about the lack of refreshments on that non-stop 12-hour journey to Wick? No problem! We'll show you how to announce "There is no Buffet on this train. However, if there had been, you would have been able to enjoy a wide selection of snacks including bacon rolls, toasted sandwiches, beefburgers, cheese-burgers, crisps, piping-hot Maxpax coffee, those big biscuits with chocolate bits stuck onto them, a selection of fine red and white vintage wines, brandy and cigars" . . . and make it seem like their fault!

Make the rich bastards travelling First Class feel small by accusing them of stealing! (We show you how to plant small pieces of Palmolive soap in their top pockets)

Make the poor bastards travelling Standard Class feel Third Class! (We give you a rule-book that says bicycles must be carried as hand-luggage)

★**FREE UNIFORM**
★**FREE TRAVEL**
★**ABSOLUTE POWER**
★**YOUR OWN TOILET-PAPER**

The British Rail Guards' Charm School – Your Chance To Get Your Own Back!

IT'S YOU THEY ANSWER TO!

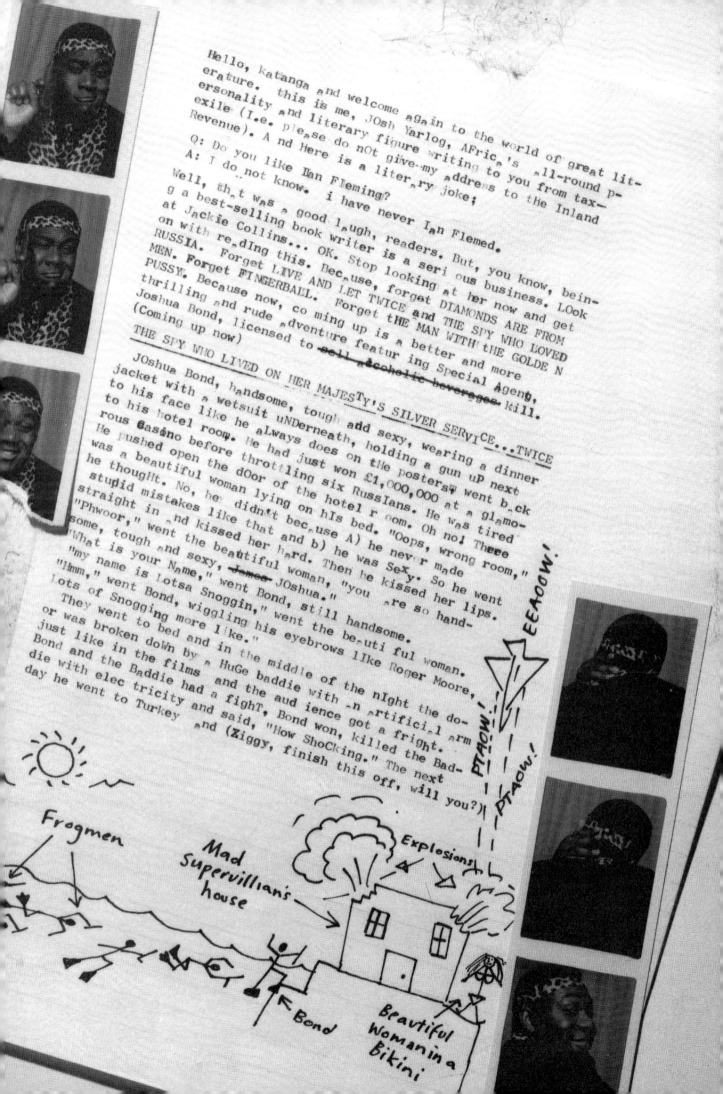

Hello, katanga and welcome again to the world of great literature. this is me, JOsh Yarlog, AFrica's all-round p-
ersonality and literary figure writing to you from tax-
exile (I.e. please do nOt give my address to tHe Inland
Revenue). A nd Here is a literary joke;

Q: Do you like Ian Fleming?

A: I do not know. i have never Ian Flemed.

Well, that was a good laugh, readers. But, you know, bein-
g a best-selling book writer is a serious business. LOok
at Jackie Collins... OK. Stop looking at her now and get
on with reading this. Because, forget DIAMONDS ARE FROM
RUSSIA. Forget LIVE AND LET TWICE and THE SPY WHO LOVED
MEN. Forget FINGERBALL. Forget tHE MAN WITH THE GOLDE N
PUSSY. Because now, co ming up is a better and more
thrilling and rude adventure featur ing Special Agent,
Joshua Bond, licensed to ~~sell alcoholic beverages~~ kill.
(Coming up now)

THE SPY WHO LIVED ON HER MAJESTy's SILVER SERVICE...TWICE

JOshua Bond, handsome, tough add sexy, wearing a dinner
jacket with a wetsuit uNDerneath, holding a gun uP next
to his face like he always does on tHe posters, went back
to his hotel room. He had just won £1,000,000 at a glamo-
rous Casino before throttling six RussIans. He was tired
He pushed open the dOor of the hotel r oom. Oh no! There
was a beautiful woman lying on hIs bed. "Oops, wrong room,"
he thougHt. No, he didn't because A) he never made
stupid mistakes like that and b) he was Sexy. So he went
straight in and kissed her hard. Then he kissed her lips.
"Phwoor," went the beautiful woman, "you are so handsome, tough and sexy," went Bond, still handsome.
"What is your Name," went Bond, ~~James~~ JOshua."
"Hmm," went Bond, wiggling his eyebrows lIke Roger Moore,
"my name is Lotsa Snoggin," went the beautiful woman.
Lots of Snogging more like."
They went to bed and in the middle of the nIght the do-
or was broken down by a HuGe baddie with an artificial arm
just like in the films and the aud ience got a fright.
Bond and the Baddie had a fighT. Bond won, killed the Baddie with elec tricity and said, "How ShoCking." The next
day he went to Turkey and (Ziggy, finish this off, will you?)

Frogmen

Mad
Supervillian's
house

Explosions!

Bond

Beautiful
Womanin a
Bikini

EEAOOW!

PTAOW! PTAOW!

Delbert Wilkins
PARTY PLANNER

"First, find somewhere that's closed at night, then hijack it – like Heathrow Airport, right?"

"Somewhere that's got plenty of parking space. The planes start trying to land again about 6am, but they have to 'stack' till we've finished, right?"

"You need a sound system that reaches every corner of the joint. But, remember, the reason the airport's closed at night is to stop disturbing the neighbours. So keep the noise down – anything up to 10 Jumbo jets is fine."

"Cos there's no flights, this tower'll be empty. So if you and your lady want to lose control, and join the half-a-mile high club, get down and get up there! Check your progress to fulfilment on the radar!"

"Put your food on here, so you've got a buffet that's *really* running, you know what I mean? But be patient, cos the snack you want will be the last one to come round. Or it may well have been sent to Peru by mistake!"

"The meals were simply delicious!"

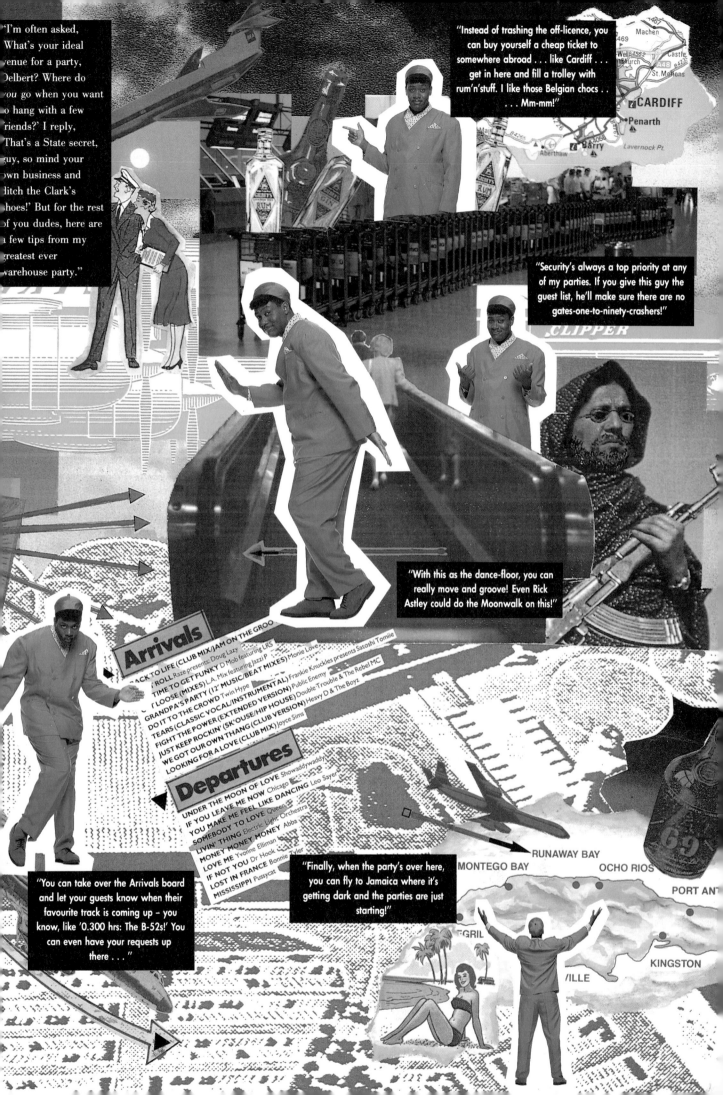

"I'm often asked, What's your ideal venue for a party, Delbert? Where do *you* go when you want to hang with a few friends?' I reply, That's a State secret, guy, so mind your own business and ditch the Clark's shoes!' But for the rest of you dudes, here are a few tips from my greatest ever warehouse party."

"Instead of trashing the off-licence, you can buy yourself a cheap ticket to somewhere abroad . . . like Cardiff . . . get in here and fill a trolley with rum'n'stuff. I like those Belgian chocs . . . . . . Mm-mm!"

"Security's always a top priority at any of my parties. If you give this guy the guest list, he'll make sure there are no gates-one-to-ninety-crashers!"

"With this as the dance-floor, you can really move and groove! Even Rick Astley could do the Moonwalk on this!"

Arrivals

BACK TO LIFE (CLUB MIX)/JAM ON THE GROO
'ROLL Raze presents, Doug Lazy
TIME TO GET FUNKY D Mob featuring LRS
LOOSE (MIXES) L.A. Mix featuring Jazzi P
GRANDPA'S PARTY (12" MUSIC/BEAT MIXES) Monie Love
DO IT TO THE CROWD Twin Hype
TEARS (CLASSIC VOCAL/INSTRUMENTAL) Frankie Knuckles presents Satoshi Tomiie
FIGHT THE POWER (EXTENDED VERSION) Public Enemy
JUST KEEP ROCKIN' (SK'OUSE/HIP HOUSE) Double Trouble & The Rebel MC
WE GOT OUR OWN THANG (CLUB VERSION) Heavy D & The Boyz
LOOKING FOR A LOVE (CLUB MIX) Joyce Sims

Departures

UNDER THE MOON OF LOVE Showaddywaddy
IF YOU LEAVE ME NOW Chicago
YOU MAKE ME FEEL LIKE DANCING Leo Sayer
SOMEBODY TO LOVE Queen
LIVIN' THING Electric Light Orchestra
MONEY MONEY MONEY Abba
LOVE ME Yvonne Elliman
IF NOT YOU Dr Hook
LOST IN FRANCE Bonnie Tyler
MISSISSIPPI Pussycat

"You can take over the Arrivals board and let your guests know when their favourite track is coming up – you know, like '0.300 hrs: The B-52s!' You can even have your requests up there . . . "

"Finally, when the party's over here, you can fly to Jamaica where it's getting dark and the parties are just starting!"

RUNAWAY BAY
MONTEGO BAY
OCHO RIOS
PORT ANT
KINGSTON
EGRIL
VILLE

CARDIFF
Penarth
Machen
St. Mellons
Aberthaw
Barry
Lavernock Pt.

CLIPPER

ARE YOU OLD
ARE YOU COLD

IF SO, YOU MAY BE ENTITLED TO A GENEROUS GOVERNMENT HYPOTHERMIA GRANT!

BUT FIRST:

CHECK YOUR CHILL FACTOR RATING AGAINST THIS MAN

This is a typical British citizen. Let's call him Mr D.

Mr D. came to us complaining of the cold in his council house, which he couldn't afford to buy. He said his bedroom was so cold his breath froze and he could read what he'd been saying in his sleep.
He applied to us for hypothermia benefit. We turned him down.

WHY?

We showed him that he wasn't maximising his body heat potential. Most body warmth escapes through the top of the head. We showed Mr D. that by wearing a hat lined with Clingfilm, baking foil and newspapers he could prevent serious heat-loss. Mr D. said he had cold feet. But he was only wearing one pair of shoes. By putting on his slippers first, then socks, then our old friends the newspapers again, then his shoes, Mr D.'s feet were as snug as a bug in a rug! And a rug is what, on our advice, he now wears next to his skin, beneath the overcoat, the undercoat, the string vest, the rope vest, the chain mail, the *Daily Mail,* the *Radio* and *TV Times* and *Country Life* (Winter Edition). Mr D. is now a happy man, with plenty to read.

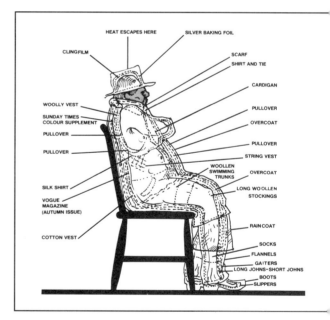

ARE YOU STILL FEELING THE COLD?

If you can prove that your blood temperature has fallen below 273° Centigrade in the last six months (including June, July and August) then we will give you

FIVE POUNDS
of margarine to smear on your chest.
Returnable within two weeks.

HELP US TO HELP YOU TO HELP YOURSELVES!

THE LENNY HENRY
FITNESS GUIDE

DISCOVERING YOUR BODY

There comes a time in a man's life when he stands on the bathroom scales and says "Who are all these other people in my trousers?" Then he looks down and realises he is alone. There's no one in his trousers but him. It's time for him to find his own personal fitness centre. What he should do next is . . . WHO AM I KIDDING? I'm talking about ME! It's me who had to keep looking round to see what the thumping noise was behind me, only to discover it was my backsides dragging along the floor!

I decided I would get fit to take better care of my heart, to have more energy for work, to make my body a temple at one with nature . . . WHO AM I KIDDING? I did it cos when I was on the beach I didn't want to look like an oil slick!

Let's face it, I was a 16-stone wimp. I wanted the good old days back, when to get fit all you had to do was walk to work instead of getting the bus and have an apple a couple of times a week instead of pudding. But now you have to hurt yourself — when they say "inch war" they mean a re-enactment of Waterloo with your bottom as the battle-field. Napoleon would take one look at mine and say "OK, we walked back from Moscow but there's no way we can get across that!"

CHOOSING THE RIGHT GYM

What I did next was went round hundreds of gyms until I found one where everyone looked as bad as me. People who started sweating when they picked up the pen to sign in. People with carrier-bag stomachs with three weeks' shopping inside — you think you've walked into the pre-natal exercise class until you realise they're all guys. They're so unhealthy, plates of chips wouldn't go near them! When they're doing aerobics their breathing sounds like bag-pipes dying of lung cancer — they're trying to touch their toes but only reaching their chins! They try to follow the steps but there's a five-hour delay between brain and body with these guys: by the time they've picked up the whole sequence of movement the instructor's gone home, been to Tenerife for his holidays, come back for a new term and thinks they're a fresh class! They're a different colour, that's all — red when they bend down, blue when they come back up.

GYM EQUIPMENT

Like a lot of gyms this one has a thing called a Nautilus Machine. It isn't a new invention, they used to have it in medieval Spain — when I'm being pulled about on it I yell out "Okay, okay, so I'm a witch!", but it won't stop. It's designed to work each muscle in your body individually — like stretching your legs out as far as they can go and then bringing them back together. You know they're stretched wide enough when a crack appears on the top of your head. Then there's a weight-and-pulley system designed to make your biceps scream — what they're screaming is "No, no — don't lift that, get a fork-lift truck!"

After I'd confessed to being Jack the Ripper, Deep Throat and the man who does the voice for Basil Brush, they finally let me go over to the exercise bikes. I got on one, started pedalling away going nowhere, and a policeman came in and nicked me for not having any lights! Ten minutes later and I'm not just sweating, my pipes have burst! People come into the gym and a giant tidal wave of sweat sweeps them out into the street again — Australians are surfing out from under my armpits! Guys are jumping on the rowing machines and doing a hundred miles an hour to get away from the killer jellyfish swimming out of my shorts!

FITNESS FOR MEN

Weight loss for guys starts as soon as they go into the changing room – they shed a couple of pounds just fighting each other to get to the mirror first. And then a couple more flicking each other with towels as they stroll around naked. Then they put on really serious T-shirts which say:

IF IT HURTS IT WORKS

NO PAIN NO GAIN

BODYBUILDERS STAY HARD LONGER

AWESOME!

BLAST IT

SUPERPUMP

I put my MARMITE SOLDIERS MAKE ME STRONG T-shirt on inside-out so nobody can read it. Then the Arnold Schwarzeneggers come in. We're talking deep-pan pizza. These guys are built like rhinos with elephant hormone injections – they've got muscles so big they need a passport to cross their legs! They have to tell air-traffic controllers if they're going to flex them! These guys won't kick sand in your face, they'll lift up the beach and tip you off. They've eaten so many mineral supplements they're walking round with the wealth of ten South American countries inside them – cut one of them open and you could give twenty miners a job.

What happens to bodybuilders who don't want to stop? They're 80 years old and want a rest, but if they don't keep working out their bodies will turn into pure lard, and they'll have to be taken to collect their pensions in frying pans. I say: if we were meant to have our veins on the outside we'd have been Stilton.

FITNESS FOR WOMEN

There are two sorts of women in the gym:

1 The ones in brand-new, matching, pink gear who come there to pose – their work-out clothes are so expensive that if you even look in their direction alarms go off and Rottweilers jump out of their leg-warmers.

They're really skinny, but it's from dieting on half a lemon and one peanut a day. Sometimes one of them comes in crying her eyes out, so depressed she tries to throw herself in front of an exercise bike and says, "Oh my God, I *looked* at a potato last night." So she does penance for it and only eats half the peanut for a month, unsalted. The gym equipment these girls work out on are the sunbeds – they think skin cancer means not having an all-over tan. And they never sweat – they come floating in on a cloud of perfume, they get high on deodorant and the corridors are blocked up with men they've never met before trying to give them flowers.

2 The serious girls – the Brigitte Nielsons who always wear black gear that's torn to shreds where their huge muscles have fought their way through, and minuscule bikini bottoms like anorexic belts for small sumo wrestlers – they're not G-strings they're A-minus strings because they've got nothing to hide. Where other women have bottoms and round bits these girls have elastic bands. Even their earlobes are lifting 20 kilo-weights!

APRÈS-GYM

When asked why they were bodybuilders 75 per cent of the 20 per cent who could speak real words said, so they could open a jar of pickled cabbage without jamming it in the door-frame. Well, I don't like pickled cabbage, and anyway I've got a girlie to do that for me, so I've decided to relax. I mean, why do we need to get fit? Giant tortoises live for 300 years and you never see them pumping iron. Every now and then I do a routine of home-exercises at home, like "The Giving–It–a–Miss–for–the–Day–System" or "The Losing–My–Gym–Clothes–Workout". And I've just about perfected The Corkscrew. Big bottoms up!

CRiCKet

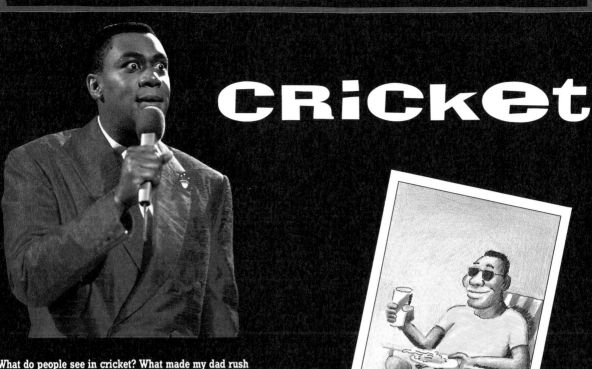

What do people see in cricket? What made my dad rush home from work, kick me out of the way and sit in front of the telly with the sound turned down and the radio turned up. . . I mean, that's crazy behaviour - specially when I'd been trying to watch Deputy Dawg and listen to Radio Caroline! "Hi, Rosko - this is Musky!" My dad'd draw the living-room curtains and send me out into the back yard, with instructions to practise my googly. So I did, with Janet Edenbrow. But cricket's so boring, right? Not cos of the rules - they're simple . . . England play the West Indies and **WE WIN!** Australia play the West Indies and **WE WIN AGAIN!** What's complicated about that? There's one thing that's really impossible to understand about cricket, and that is: what do those banners mean that English fans sit up all night making? They say things like **"BIG BIRD'S GOING TO LAND ON HIS BOTHAM ON THE GOWER PENINSULA".** Twenty yards of incomprehensible joke, right? It needs a subtitle: "The Person Sitting Underneath This Is a Twat". West Indian supporters don't believe in banners - if we did they'd just say **"DIE!"** Have you ever wondered why the West Indies don't have a nuclear defence system? We don't need one - we've got **MALCOLM MARSHALL.** It's great listening to the commentators when Marshall's running in to bowl at one of the England batsmen . . . "And Gooch takes guard as Marshall comes in off his short run . . . he's got a line of sandbags stretching from square-leg to cover-point and the roll of barbed wire has been brought up to silly mid-on . . . Gooch lowers his visor, adjusts his breast-plate and fiddles nervously with his chain-mail . . . as Marshall approaches the wicket Gooch raises his bat above the trench . . . Marshall bowls - and it's gone straight through Gooch, there's a sticky hole just below his ribs, and it whistles past the wicket-keeper's ear, taking the other one with it, and now it's out of the ground and past the Zoo and up the Seven Sisters Road and while we wait for the ball to be retrieved by the coastguards I think it's time for some cake, don't you Johnners?" . . . Ian Botham's got the right idea: while the England fans are unpacking their chutney sandwiches and their car-rugs and the England team are having their pep-talk - "Don't forget men, it's not losing that counts, it's *how* we lose - surrender gracefully. Invite them to dinner afterwards. Offer them your wives. So, tally-ho, boxes on and over the top!" - Ian's in the West Indies dressing-room, having a little smoke and a drink with Viv and the guys. A bit of fisticuffs outside the disco afterwards - he's an honorary dude! So maybe next time he's playing for England against the West Indies at the Oval and the sun's warm, I'll go down there, and try and work out how you can bowl a Chinaman when they haven't even got a team? I'll take a banner, and pretend my old man's holding the other end: **"WHAT WOULD WE BE LIKE IF WE PRACTISED?"**

HOW CRUCIAL are YOU?

Delbert Wilkins sets you 20 questions to enable you to assess your very own cruciality rating – tick one of three boxes then check how you've scored on the Delbertometer at the end of the questionnaire.

1. Do You Have A Crucial Name? Is It:
a: Delbert ☐
b: Winston ☐
c: Other ☐

2. What Time Do You Get Up?
a: When my body says 'Go For It!' ☐
b: When I have to go to work ☐
c: When my Mum makes me ☐

3. When You Stand Naked Before The Mirror In The Morning, Does Your Reflection Say:
a: 'How about some life insurance?' ☐
b: 'Why are you doing a handstand?' ☐
c: 'Yo!' ☐

4. Where Do You Keep Your Clothes?
a: Hanging neatly in a wardrobe ☐
b: In a Security Vault at Bejam ☐
c: In a Bin Bag ☐

5. Where Do You Buy Your Clothes?
a: Giorgio Armani ☐
b: Armani & Navy ☐
c: Freemans Catalogue ☐

6. How Much Do You Spend On Clothes?
a: Under £50 a month ☐
b: Over £50 a sock ☐
c: Nothing – they pay me to wear them! ☐

7. When You Walk Down The Street, Do People:
a: Get down on all fours and lick the pavement in front of you ☐
b: Thrust their small change at you ☐
c: Laugh ☐

8. Does Your Car Have:
a: A tax disc ☐
b: Mushrooms growing on the bodywork ☐
c: Its own lane on the motorway ☐

9. Describe Your Record Collection:
a: Mainly Rick Astley and all the other Stock, Aitken and Waterman platters – they're so funky! ☐
b: So big it's got to be rehoused by the council ☐
c: Yah, I'm heavily into opera just now actually – except they can't fit Pavarotti onto a compact disc ☐

10. If Someone Approaches You Aggressively On The Street, Do You:
a: Say 'Come outside and say that' ☐
b: Suggest he checks that his Organ Donor card is filled in before *he is!* ☐
c: Ask him to take the whistle out of his mouth and show you his warrant card ☐

11. You're Out With Your Lady And It Starts Raining. Do You:
a: Give her your umbrella so she can hold it over you ☐
b: Take off your Hugo Boss jacket and put it over her head ☐
c: Take shelter in a Spud-U-Like and stay for a meal ☐

12. What Is Your Favourite TV Programme?
a: That's My Dog ☐
b: The Delbert Wilkins Show ☐
c: Frank Bough on Sky ☐

13. What Magazines Do You Read?
a: Other peoples' ☐
b: Q, i-D, GQ, 19, 20/20 ☐
c: The Tablet, Chat, My Freezer, Jane's Fighting Ships ☐

14. Has Your Favourite Restaurant Got:
a: Photographers outside ☐
b: Health inspectors inside ☐
c: A really exciting new chef from Bulgaria, apparently ☐

15. Someone Offers You Cocaine At A Party. Do You:
a: Make a citizens' arrest ☐
b: Cut it with your platinum Amex card ☐
c: Tell him your nostrils are a snow-free environmental zone ☐

16. A Woman Claims You Are The Father Of Her Baby. Do You:
a: Show her your vasectomy certificate ☐
b: Get her to point you out in an identity parade ☐
c: Marry her ☐

17. Where Did You Spend Your Last Foreign Holiday?
a: Departure Lounge at Luton Airport ☐
b: Peckham ☐
c: Orbiting the Earth in the Space Shuttle ☐

18. You Are About To Be Wheel-Clamped. Do You:
a: Tell them there's a bomb in the car ☐
b: Kill them ☐
c: Buy another car ☐

19. What Is Your Favourite Drink?
a: A pint of Baadermeinhofmeister ☐
b: A cup of Nescafe made by Gareth Hunt ☐
c: A Brixton Sunrise – part tequila, part Red Stripe, and the rest you can never remember! ☐

20. What Time Do You Go To Bed?
a: After *Newsnight* ☐
b: When I've cleaned my shoes ready for the morning ☐
c: When my body says 'Chill!' ☐

Now See How You Rate!

Bad luck, guy! True Cruciality means not having to do any dumb tests like this to find out whether you are or not – one instinctively knows when one is crucial! And now people are laughing and saying 'Look at that lemon reading a book upside down!' You score Zero Points! We're talking Turkey in the Eurovision Song Contest!

WARNING!
WARNING!
WARNING!
WARNING!

The Proprietors and Legal Advisers of BLACK EXECUTIVE Hair Care Products, have issued an urgent warning to all purchasers of BLACK EXECUTIVE grooming kits and hair oils, that there may, in certain cases, be an adverse reaction to the use of certain BLACK EXECUTIVE products due to a crop-dusting error in the Bald Knob, Arkansas region. But there is no need to panic! Those at risk fall mainly in the 16-65 black, male age-group. If you feel concerned then take the following action: do NOT use any non-BLACK EXECUTIVE products. DO write to the specially-appointed:

**BLACK EXECUTIVE OMBUDSMAN,
C/O NORIEGA TOWER,
AVENIDA DE LOS LOSCAUSES,
GRAND CONMAN ISLANDS.**

WELL-HARD

A W.H. Allen/Virgin Books
Production of a
Lenworth J. Henry Film

They Were a Gang
With One Ruthless
Purpose – to Make
You Die Laughing!!!

Written by: **Lenny Henry, Stan Hey, Andrew Nickolds and Kim Fuller**
Additional Material: **James Hendrie, Anne Caulfield and Geoff Atkinson**
Edited by: **ANDREW NICKOLDS and STAN HEY**
Executive Producer: **Cat Ledger**
Assistant to Executive Producer: **Judith Murray**
Director of Photography: **Trevor Leighton**
Additional Photography: **Clive Helm**

Art Director: **Phil Healey**
Production Team: **Paul Crome, Lesley Jennings, Paul Sudron, Nick Renn and Ros Ormston**
Costume Design: **Sharon Lewis and Clodagh Scott**
Make-up Design: **Sally Sutton**
Illustrations by: **Lin Jammet, John Bradley, Frances Lloyd, Mick Armson, Alan Preston, Paul McLoughlin and Phil Healey**

Out on Video soon
the Film of the Book of the T.V. series

Bridal outfits kindly provided by Pronuptia. Photographs courtesy of Barnaby's, BBC Enterprises, Format and Rex Features